TRUE STORIES OF FRONTIER WOMEN

BY DIXIE BOYLE

Dedication

Preface

Epilogue

Dedication:

I would like to dedicate this book to the memory of Dorothy Neeley Cole. She loved history and was always more than willing to share with those who sought information. I do not want her or her contributions to the history of Mountainair, New Mexico to ever be forgotten.

Many an afternoon Dorothy and I sat in her living room at Rancho Bonito and talked about history. Not just local history but about the history of the American West. I haven't found too many people who have read as many books as I have about the settlement and opening of the American Frontier, but Dorothy's appetite for western history matched my own. We talked about Elizabeth Custer, Molly Goodnight and Susan McSween; as well as, the Civil War, Jesse James, the Oregon Trail, the murder of Crazy Horse and how the discovery of gold changed the west.

One of the last times I saw Dorothy she gave me the book *In Time of Harvest* by John Sinclair. It is the classic story of homesteading and pinto bean farming in Torrance County. I had never read or even heard of the book before, but soon saw why Dorothy would want to pass it on to someone who would appreciate it. The characters in the book remind me of many of the old timers I heard stories about while growing up near Mountainair.

Dorothy was truly loved by the Mountainair community. The chapel where her memorial was held was packed to overflowing as people of all ages and races attended. There were newcomers to the area, as well as the descendants of those who had homesteaded the land a century earlier. They all wanted to show their love and pay their last respects to Dorothy. She was fair and honest with everyone she met and significantly contributed to the preservation of the history of the area. She was quite the classy lady and an eloquent speaker. She will be missed!

**Dorothy & her cousin Henrian on the
Family ranch circa 1950
Dorothy Cole Photo**

An irreplaceable link to Mountainair's past was lost on Saturday, March 5, 2016, with the passing of Dorothy Neeley Cole. For decades, she was referred to as the town historian. She freely shared old photographs and documentation she had collected with genealogists, writers and those researching local history. She loved the history of Mountainair and the pinto bean era and was passionate about its preservation.

Dorothy naturally assumed the role of town historian when she returned to the area twenty-seven years ago after traveling the world and living a life far removed from the small family ranch near Mountainair she had called home. Her memories of the old bean fields once prevalent throughout Torrance County and her country roots drew her home again where she continued to preserve the stories of her people.

"I have always loved history and have collected old photos and stories as long as I can remember," Dorothy stated in an interview, "I especially love the pinto bean era and the history of ranching that followed, as both are part of my history."

Dorothy's parents Doc and Johnnie Belle Neeley, moved to New Mexico from Muleshoe, Texas in the 1930s and operated a sawmill in the Gallinas Mountains near Corona before leasing the land that would become the family ranch southeast of Mountainair.

"My dad was not a farmer, but he often hauled pinto beans to market for them and our ranch was surrounded by bean farms," Dorothy pointed out. "My parents found ways to make a living by ranching and driving a rural school bus route. There was a lot of activity around Mountainair during the pinto bean years."

She wrote and directed a musical entitled *Diamonds in the Field.* It is a tribute to the pinto bean farmers and their legacy in the Estancia Valley. Not only did she compose songs of this era in Mountainair's history, but she convinced a few descendants of other farmers to do the same. They performed their songs to an audience of six hundred people at the Robert Saul Community Center in Mountainair at their debut performance on August 4, 2001.

The title of the musical came from a song Dorothy wrote that referred to the pinto bean crop as diamonds. She wrote, "I'll work that field and hoe them weeds, row after row come harvest it will be a diamond mine. . .Got that wagon loaded now with diamonds from the field."

"I must admit, there are times when I find myself searching the landscape for the old bean fields and for a brief moment I actually wonder where they went," Dorothy said. "You can see them in places if you look hard enough but then in others they have totally disappeared. The land doesn't seem right without them."

Dorothy graduated from Mountainair High School in 1957 and moved to Denver, Colorado for a career with the Mountain Bell Telephone Company. She often traveled as required by her job, going as far as Russia, and ran in the New York City Marathon. However, Dorothy remained a country girl in her heart and in 1989 when her working career ended, she returned home to Mountainair.

She bought Pop Shaffer's historic ranch called Rancho Bonito south of Mountainair and lived in the rock caretaker's cottage built by Shaffer on the site. She painted and renovated the buildings on the ranch and gave historical tours of the property. Dorothy knew Pop Shaffer personally and recounted interesting stories about his life and character when visitors stopped to view the unique art-deco style ranch he had created.

Not only was Dorothy a chronicler of history, but also of the music making up the era. Music was an important part of her childhood. Dances were held most Saturday nights, either at one of the country schoolhouses dotting the land, or hosted by one of the bean farmers. People dressed up in their best flour sack clothing and danced and visited all night. Dorothy learned to "pick" the guitar as well as dance at these country musicals, preparing her to compose her own songs and to organize public musicals and concerts.

There was little money for entertainment, so those cultivating the bean fields provided their own. Many traveled long distances to attend the country dances and brought dinner and cake for a midnight meal. The entire family attended the Saturday night musicals. Dorothy described these musicals in *Diamonds in the Field,* "Those get-togethers were something. The women always had something good to eat. When we kids got sleepy, we'd just lay on some blankets or coats over in a corner and go to sleep. Those are some of the best memories I have of growing up."

Dorothy explained that much of the music she learned while growing up was handed down by the local musicians. "We didn't keep up with the new music or top forty, as we had to save the batteries of the radio to listen to news every couple of days," she wrote. "Sometimes we'd get to hear the Grand Old Opry, but not very often."

Almost a century has passed since Mountainair was known as the Pinto Bean Capital of the World. Caravans of wagons are no longer seen, creeping through the bean fields laden with pinto beans on their way to the railhead in Mountainair during harvest time. The old bean fields have all but vanished except as memories of those who helped to harvest the crops as children.

"I dearly love the history of the old bean fields and the interesting characters who farmed them," Dorothy stated when asked why this history was so important to her. "The farmers of that era worked hard but knew how to have a good time when the work was done and those times make good memories."

Dorothy felt strongly about the old stories and photos, "I do not want the history to be forgotten. It is important for this history to be passed on, as the old-timers are all gone now. The way to truly preserve history is to keep telling it, writing about it, and sharing it, as there will always be an interest in local history."

The pinto bean farmers were a close-knit group. They harvested crops together, celebrated at one another's weddings and mourned at their funerals. Dancing all night at the country dances was a main source of entertainment for the farmers. They helped each other endure the drought years and failure of their pinto bean crops. This era in Mountainair's history has long passed, but because of local historians like Dorothy Cole, Mountainair's history will not be forgotten, and neither will she.

Preface:

It is often disappointing how few accurate facts are available about the women settling the American West. In many cases, the only hints of their pasts are faded photographs, birth or death records in a family Bible, a tarnished locket or an unidentified grave along the remnants of a lonely wagon road. Women may have settled on the frontier in smaller numbers than their male counterparts but they all arrived on the frontier for many of the same reasons: a desire for independence, a thirst for adventure and a break from the Victorian mores of the era.

Unknown Frontier Women
Photo — Author's Collection

Some of these women made the trek in covered wagons with their families to build new lives, while a few struck out alone. Many opened boarding houses and cafes and others taught in one-room schoolhouses and raised money to build churches and mercantile stores. Of course, there were some who made the move in order to hide from their pasts or with hopes of making a quick fortune. Whatever their reason, these female pioneers contributed enormously to civilizing the wild and untamed frontier.

The American West was largely a man's world. Men in some cases outnumbered the women as high as 25-1 and in the goldfields of California and Alaska the number could go even higher. The first stories emerging about this era were written about men by other men while history about the women is often missing, untrue, incomplete or entirely ignored.

However, there are thousands of interesting women who inhabited the American frontier and their stories have never really been told. Amongst them were women writers, former slaves, Native Americans, brothel owners, pilots, fire lookouts, artists and others who made their own contributions to the history of their time. These early women settling the frontier were often as tough as the men as they struggled to survive and prosper. Many of them had grown up on the frontier and knew no other type of life.

Particularly inspiring are the stories of countless women homesteaders who flocked to the plains states in order to homestead and eventually own their own land. Women have not always had the right to own land. Women lived in one-room shacks with few conveniences, and they often endured floods, fires, insect infestations, Indian attacks and more in an effort to prove up on their homesteads.

In the settlement of the American West, women often experienced terrifying attacks by Native American tribes living in the area. Some watched their entire family massacred or their children abducted and endured the heartbreak of never knowing what had become of them. Unless someone has experienced a home invasion, the terror and isolation felt by these women is almost impossible for modern women to understand. It was definitely a challenging time for women trying to make a life for themselves on the American frontier.

Women used different forms of transportation to travel to the frontier. Many came in covered wagons, while others took river boats, trains, rode horse-back, or even arrived in army ambulances. There were those who rode the train as far as possible and then continued either by stage or rented horses to complete the journey. Others walked the entire way pushing hand carts, fueled by their obsession with finding a new home and way of life. It was not an easy life, but there were generally more unconventional opportunities available to those women with the courage and knowledge to survive on the frontier.

Woman Riding the Train
Dorothy Cole Photo

The first women to arrive on the frontier in any great numbers were those establishing brothels, cat and parlor houses and saloons. They came by the thousands to mining and cattle towns where they could meet men desiring their services. They brought their looks and brains and hoped they would have enough money to return to a more respectable life in six months or a year, while others enjoyed the life and made a good profit from their businesses. Some never left the frontier while others were buried in unmarked graves in the prostitute section of a lonely cemetery.

Many unconventional women were a success as Wild West and rodeo stars and traveled the "circuit" while performing in front of large crowds throughout the United States. They were the darlings of the rodeo world and many spectators attended only so they could see their favorite stars and their daring stunts. These stars also performed in vaudeville and silent movies making a name in Hollywood, where they even had to provide their own stunt horses and equipment.

Many women thrived on the American frontier, because they were free from the Victorian mores and standards they had been forced to adhere to, and they were judged on their own merits and not those of their husbands, fathers or brothers. The West was a place where women could take advantage of the opportunity to start over, make a new life for themselves and prosper on their own.

Women crossing the frontier in wagon trains had a long, hard dangerous journey before reaching their destinations. There were those who turned back when the rigors of the trail became too much for them or their livestock and equipment, while others died or were killed along the route. Many women perished in river crossings or were thrown under the wagon and run over when their skirts were caught in the wagon wheel. There was quicksand, rattlesnakes and wild animals, but the one tragedy the women dreaded the most was to be attacked by Native Americans waiting for them along the trail.

Those women who spent years in captivity with Native Americans often wanted to remain with the tribe when they were rescued. Yet, they were forced to return to their families where the relationships were never the same as they had been before the abduction. Living amongst the Indians had changed them and they became accustomed to a more unconventional, unrestricted lifestyle. Typically they did not assimilate well back into American society, as many of the women were ostracized thereafter and it would have been better for them to have remained with their Indian captives.

It would be the same for Native American women who were taken from their own tribe and raised in an alien culture such as Lost Bird of the Lakota tribe. If Lost Bird had been allowed to remain with her Lakota relatives after the massacre at Wounded Knee, she may have had a more peaceful and satisfying life and felt the acceptance of her people. Instead she was passed between her adoptive parents and ended up performing in vaudeville and Wild West shows portraying a caricature of her people when they freely roamed the Great Plains.

Unidentified Victorian Black Women Circa 1890
Photo — Author's Collection

Ironically, African-American women arriving on the frontier during its early years were often totally accepted into the frontier communities of the time and judged by their merits not their race. The West was a much more forgiving place than the southern states and even states in the north after the Civil War. There were African-American women who drove stagecoaches, opened their own boarding houses and eating establishments; as well as, those who became mid-wives and frequently administered the only medical treatment available for hundreds of miles.

After establishing homesteads and farms on the frontier, it was tragic when families had to leave their homes due to drought and economic depressions. The Great Depression and drought years that followed were extremely difficult for those families trying to support themselves on the frontier. Many had to leave their homes behind and seek work elsewhere. There were those who moved to California and other areas where they could find work and then return to their farms when the drought years ended. Many traveled across the border into Mexico and found employment and experienced a different culture for a few years until they returned to the United States.

At the turn of the twentieth century, there were women who sought employment in fields that had traditionally belonged to men such as fire lookouts, ranch hands and airplane pilots. These first courageous women would open the way for women throughout the frontier seeking the same type of employment. The Victorian Era was passing and with it more opportunities and a less restrictive lifestyle for the women inhabiting the American West.

Cecilia Anderson – First Hillsboro Peak Fire Lookout Circa 1921--U.S. Forest Service Photo

Women artists and writers began to discover the frontier and its history and landscapes. Artists soon found the "light" in New Mexico was perfect for photographers, artists and painters and their subject matter was often unique and different from what they had painted in the past. Mabel Dodge Luhan and Georgia O'Keeffe would be the first to arrive but thousands would soon follow and discover what remained of America's frontier.

D.H. Lawrence, his wife Frieda, Andrew Dashburg, Ansel Adams, Mary Austin, Willa Cather and others flocked to Mabel Dodge Luhan's wonderful house in Taos where they discussed literature and art movements while working on their own writing and paintings. Luhan often invited people to her Taos hacienda.

Artists discovered Mountainair in central New Mexico over thirty years ago and have helped keep the town alive, much as other groups have done throughout the state. They have committed time and money to renovate many of the original buildings in Mountainair bringing the town back to its original look.

The book will cover the history of women making up America's frontier and their contributions to the history of the American West. Many may remain anonymous, while others went by nicknames and their true identities have not been discovered. But, there were others whose history was documented and preserved for future historians and writers. Researchers are only now discovering the importance these women had on the communities where they settled.

Opal, Dee & Bernice Swope in the 1920s
Author's Grandma Opal & Her Sisters
Photo: Author's Collection

***

Note from author: I have spent a lifetime reading about the adventuresome women who inhabited the American West. Many times throughout my life I have felt I was born at least a hundred years too late. I think I would have loved to see the Native American tribes during their heyday and the buffalo overflowing the plains. One way to discover how the women really lived and survived during these years is by reading their diaries, journals and family histories.

I became interested in the various women making up this book at different times throughout my life. I started a folder over twenty years ago where I stored old photographs I came across and stories I collected about women; as well as, interesting facts and references I could explore when I had more time. While living and traveling throughout the American West, I soon discovered there were endless stories about women just waiting to be told.

In the 1990s, I worked as the Education Director at the Adams Museum in Deadwood, South Dakota. In addition to developing educational programs and visiting the local schools, I was also in charge of an exhibit on prostitution. I soon found I was fascinated with this time in our history and I still cannot resist a story or two about the soiled doves who made history over a century ago. I was especially interested in those women who worked in the high-class parlor houses of the era and the red-light districts found in different regions of the United States.

While growing up on a ranch in New Mexico, I frequently read about those first women bronc and trick riders who performed in rodeos and Wild West shows. I am sure a good many girls growing up on ranches thought about becoming a rodeo star. I started to collect old post cards and photographs of Prairie Rose Henderson and others I thought might make an interesting book one day. While living in Wyoming, I visited the Buffalo Bill Cody Museum and was impressed with the history and artifacts I discovered there. Women were instrumental in running their own ranches, especially during an era when it was not thought proper for a woman, and many went on to become role models for the independent ranch women that followed.

I always felt I gained my sense of adventure from the women in my family. There are women who would not agree to follow their husbands to a foreign country. My grandmother, mother and aunt all went to Mexico to live during the Great Depression and enjoyed the adventure of being in a new country and learning the customs of other people. They often talk about those years as something they would never have missed even though the food was often bad and violence common throughout the country.

When I graduated from high school I wanted to teach in a one-room schoolhouse. There were only a few left by this time in Wyoming and Montana and now they are all closed. So any book I would write on women would have to include a pioneer teacher or two and I found the perfect one to include in the book –Mabel Sibley Jones from Wilmington, Delaware.

Those women captured and living amongst the native people has been an interest of mine since childhood. It would have been terrifying and heartbreaking to leave your family behind and be forced to accompany strangers into the wilderness. I am sure as the years went by, you would forget your native language and customs especially if you were taken at a young age.

When I lived in the Black Hills in Wyoming I discovered the story of Lucretia Marchbanks, a former slave from Tennessee, and was impressed that she was able to purchase her own ranch at that time in history. She raised cattle and horses and lived on the ranch for the remainder of her life. Before purchasing her ranch, she made a name as a cook and honest woman and she was quite popular among those settling the Black Hills area.

I was a child the first time I visited Capilla Peak Fire Lookout in New Mexico's Manzano Mountains, and I decided that one day I would work as a fire lookout. No one told me a fire lookout only works during the summer months and spends endlessly long hours and days in the fire tower. But, it was definitely the job for me. In the beginning of the history of the U.S. Forest Service, women were not considered qualified for the job of a fire lookout.

Not only did these early fire lookouts spot fires but they had to ride horse-back or hike miles to locate and extinguish the fires they reported. Men built and staffed the first fire lookouts, but by the turn of the twentieth century more and more women were being hired for this position. It was a surprise for some that women made excellent and dedicated fire lookouts, as they did not mind spending weeks alone on a mountaintop and making friends with the animals living nearby.

Many of my friends are artists, and for the most part they live a peaceful life working on their art projects and attending art exhibits and shows. I have read Mabel Dodge Luhan's books about her discovery of New Mexico and the Taos area. She made a major change in her life by moving to Taos at a time when there were no hotels or much of a town. She embraced the culture and the people of New Mexico and spent the rest of her life in the state. She was extremely outspoken and forceful in her feelings about art and life in general. Countless artists have made their home in New Mexico and have been good for the state both economically and socially.

Victorian Woman Ellen Gerhardt
Photo—Author's Collection

Throughout the book I will often refer to the Victorian Era. This era in our history began in the 1880s and was mostly gone by the 1920s. It was an era influenced by the reign of Queen Victoria from England that dictated to women how they should always act in a lady-like manner. This mainly related to the upper class but all women were subject to ridicule if they over-stepped what was expected of them.

They were not to own their own businesses or frequent saloons and dancehalls. They rode horse-back only in a sidesaddle and attired in the cumbersome riding habits of the era. There was an unwritten set of rules that respectable women were expected to follow.

Women of the higher class were referred to as ladies and they set the standards for other women even those living on the American frontier. Women were expected to be quiet and modest in their language and were taught the strictest manners from a young age. Women were always to remain in the background and only interfere in a quiet and helpful manner.

Many women resented the moral standards imposed upon them and were relieved upon discovering the standards on the American frontier were much more lenient. With the inception of the Roaring Twenties and the flapper generation, the outdated standards of the Victorian Era became obsolete.

I hope you enjoy these stories about women as much as I have enjoyed researching and writing about them.

Marilyn Conway's Relatives in the 1920s
Marilyn Conway Photo

Chapter One—Old West Saloon Girls, Madams & Bodegas

The American public has long been fascinated with the history of the American frontier and the characters inhabiting its landscape and first settlements. Parlor houses, brothels, flamboyant madams and those women who were either desperate or brave enough to settle in isolated areas were often the first females to grace the history of the American frontier.

There were women who followed the military expeditions, cattle drives, boom towns and helped settle those first frontier towns that provided few conveniences. In the early years of settlement, soiled doves received more respect than they did twenty years later when reform movements swept the country and more respectable women accompanied their husbands and fathers to the frontier. Ladies of the night were soon shunned by the more respected element and placed in red-light districts where movement outside the tenderloin was restricted.

Frontier madams were typically known for building large, Victorian-style mansions where they hired jazz bands, served steak dinners and hired the best-looking women they could find to staff their parlor houses. These women were set up in style, and were required to learn manners, conduct themselves as ladies and in some cases even learned to speak French.

Some parlor house madams even gave their girls newspapers and books to read, so they could converse with the gentlemen who frequented their establishments. These businesses commonly had a gambling casino, saloon, ballroom and smoking parlor for the men. The furnishings were elegant and inviting.

These early madams often used their fortunes to help others, nursed community members through health epidemics, found homes for orphan children and stray animals, plus sent money back home to support elderly parents and siblings. They socialized with the mayor, sheriff and others who were political powers at the time. They were not afraid to voice their opinions on injustice or morality.

In today's society where women are accustomed to seeking employment in almost any field they desire, it is difficult to understand how very limited the opportunities were for women during the Victorian Era. They did not have the right to vote or own property, and in many cases were not considered respectable unless they lived under the umbrella of a father, husband, son or brother. Women were not encouraged to run their own businesses but were expected to remain at home and take care of the family, or find respectable employment outside the home as domestics. Even today, these jobs remain some of the lowest paying and least appreciated positions available.

There were few opportunities for women to make sufficient money on their own. Some women joined the trade because they needed to make quick money and then moved on; while others enjoyed men, drinking and the excitement of living a more colorful lifestyle. If these women had enough gumption, they could earn a fortune and then head back home before their reputations were entirely ruined.

Establishments during this era were often more than just houses of prostitution, but served as meeting places where drinking, dancing, gambling and other activities were enjoyed upstairs, and many times breakfast was served before the men left the brothel at dawn. The ladies of the night would sometimes provide baths for their favorite clients.

The population of women settling on the frontier was slow to grow in the early years, as life in the West was crude and primitive with little law enforcement and men often made up 99% of the population. According to Jane MacKell in the book *Red Light Women of the Rocky Mountains,* men significantly outnumbered the women on the Colorado frontier. She wrote, "In 1860 the ratio of men to women in Colorado was sixteen to one. In other areas the ratio was even higher."

Historians often question why so many women became involved in prostitution during the settlement of the American frontier. In many ways, it was a lot more glamorous than operating a laundry or boarding house and the pay was a lot better. A good many women became used to wearing expensive gowns, jewelry and discussing politics with powerful men.

Prostitutes went by many names. Several popular euphemisms included soiled doves, women of the night, sporting girl and prairie nymph. These early working girls lived in what were commonly called a bawdy house, disorderly house, cat house, parlor house or house of ill repute.

The typical day for most prostitutes started around noon and ended in the early morning hours. The girls tried to service as many men as possible so they could make the most money during the hours the parlor house was open. When they were not performing in upstairs rooms, they were drinking, dancing and encouraging men to play cards and listen to music. During the daylight hours, the women were left to their own devices. Many of the women slept until late in the day, but there were others who enjoyed reading and learning new dance steps when few people were in the brothel.

A common fee for their services was anywhere from fifty cents to fifty dollars, depending upon the situation, location and specific prostitute and man wanting sexual services. Unless extra services were requested and paid for upfront, the sexual transaction lasted only a few minutes to half an hour. There were favored customers who might receive extra time, but the working girls were expected to make their nightly tally and share it with the madam.

Shady ladies working in parlor houses averaged between 3-6 customers an evening. Those unfortunate ladies of the night who worked in smaller cribs closer to the street averaged as many as 20-25 men during an evening shift. Many houses required cleaning of both the prostitute and the client before the transaction, while others left that up to the individual prostitute.

Many of the soiled doves did not remain at the same location for the duration of their careers, as they thought it was bad for business. They often traveled in groups or with a couple gamblers for protection and went on an informal circuit during the summer months if weather and time permitted. The women even took vacations where they could visit major cities and pretend to be respectable women enjoying a vacation together.

Brothels were not quite as extravagant as the parlor houses, but rooms were provided upstairs for companionship, drinks were normally served downstairs, with smoking and gambling on the side. These houses provided luxuries not often seen on the frontier, even if the customers had to pay outrageous prices for the privilege of visiting them. The one-room cribs and small houses opening onto the street where ladies of the night could make a quick turnaround were not as desirable as the brothels for working prostitutes of the era. Crib girls were considered higher on the ladder than dancehall girls. Those saloon girls who were unable to leave the profession were often found working as street walkers and begging any man they encountered to take them home for a small fee. If a lady of the night reached this stage, she would soon be found dead from an overdose of morphine or heroin and later buried in an unmarked grave.

When brothels and saloons first opened on the American frontier, dance hall girls most often were the ones to entice the men into spending their money. These women were not prostitutes but hired as dancers, although their reputations were ruined just as quickly as those performing upstairs. It was not thought appropriate for women to dance in bars and gambling houses during the Victorian Era.

Hurdy-gurdy houses or dancehalls was another establishment where people went to dance on the frontier. According to Anne Seagraves in the book *Soiled Doves Prostitution in the Early West*, "These houses were usually long, narrow frame buildings with a bar at one end and dance floors on the other, and a hallway with several rooms near the rear. The rooms were rented to customers who wanted more than a dance, and to the hurdy-gurdy girls who chose to entertain a man after working hours. None of these girls were prostitutes; most earned a good salary from dancing and serving drinks.

Men bought dance tickets entitling them to only one dance with a woman of their choice. In other establishments, the men had to buy a certain number of drinks in order to have a dance with one of the women. The women earned their money though, as they often danced between 25-50 times during an evening. On a good night, they could make between one and two hundred dollars and not do much more than dance and visit with lonely men.

As the population increased on the American frontier and more men brought their wives, mothers and daughters with them, the number of laws limiting where and when houses of prostitution could operate and who worked in them increased. Red-light districts were organized where prostitution was allowed, but in some cases the women were almost held prisoner there. Most red-light districts were found near the railroad tracks and town depot.

According to Jan MacKell in the book *Red Light Women of the Rocky Mountains*, "Fancy parlor houses were more prevalent in the early years, before the ratio of men to women began to equalize. As more women arrived in the West, the need for parlor houses slowly diminished and the number of single-cribs rose." Men were only interested in quick sex and no dancing and conversation like in the years before the civilized women moved to the American frontier.

Although a few prostitutes came from wealthy families on the East Coast, the majority of them came from poor homes on the American frontier from the western states where they had grown up and worked. Anne Butler talks about prostitution in the book *Daughters of Joy, Sisters of Misery Prostitution in the American West 1865-90*. "These early prostitutes came from the poorest group of women on the frontier."

The sporting girls represented women of all races. There were freed black slaves who opened brothels and did quite well as independent businesswomen. Chinese women were often forced into prostitution before escaping or dying in captivity.

In the 1890s in Cripple Creek, Colorado when the discovery of gold brought the entire nation out of the Depression, the red-light district stretched over five miles. Women of all nationalities worked in the brothels. In Rawhide, Nevada the red-light district comprised a four mile area in 1908 with between five and six hundred sporting girls working the area.

Fancy parlor houses and brothels thrived on the American frontier for a twenty year period when cowboys, outlaws, buffalo hunters, military scouts, railroad workers and men making their mark on the frontier appreciated and wanted their services. Although, many of these women were unconventional for their time, they fit in the unconventional West. The history left behind by these sporting girls gives us an idea of the wild lifestyle they all shared.

Only now are historians starting to appreciate the contributions of these women of questionable morals. Accounts of their lives were left behind in diaries, newspaper articles, photographs found in scrapbooks kept by madams as well as in family albums. The early newspaper articles often made fun of the prostitutes and their plights and treated them in a burlesque manner when discussing their deaths and exploits in the paper.

The true identities of these women may never be known, as they guarded the true circumstances of their pasts. They often made up elaborate stories, as many of them never told their families back home what type of business they were conducting. Most times their families never discovered the type of life they led.

Although, the names of these soiled doves may be lost to history, many of their nicknames and aliases have remained leaving a hint to their pasts. These women had a certain style and were participants in a time of excitement, opportunity and growth. They will never return to the isolated plains and mountains of the western United States, but the stories they left behind in these first communities will remain.

Those prostitutes lucky enough to gain employment in one of the fancy parlor houses dotting the American frontier were the fortunate ones. They made the most money, dealt with the upper-crust of customers, and often had loyal madams who took care of them and dressed them in expensive gowns and jewelry.

The girls who worked in these houses were usually the youngest and best looking. Madams running parlor houses only hired girls who were in their late teens or early twenties. These young girls were schooled in the art of seduction, as well as being taught manners and how to dress properly. They were also able to discuss classic books, politics and issues of concern to gentleman of the day.

One of the first luxurious and tasteful parlor houses in the United States was founded by the Everleigh sisters in Chicago. It is believed they were born in Kentucky where they were both married young. The marriages did not last and the two sisters had a brief stage career before founding the Everleigh Club, a high-class parlor house that severed champagne in addition to steak and lobster dinners.

During the 1898 Trans-Mississippi Exposition the sisters first tried their luck at a career in high-class prostitution. A fifty dollar entrance fee was charged to those men wanting admittance to the establishment. Those entering were also required to have either a letter of recommendation or a formal calling card.

***

Of all the fancy parlor houses making money and providing entertainment with style, there were four that were considered the most tasteful and classy of all parlor houses found throughout the American frontier. They were Madam Palmer's Gentleman's Club in El Paso, Texas; Fanny Porter's Hell's Half-Acre in the red-light district of San Antonio, Texas; the Old Homestead House in Cripple Creek, Colorado whose infamous madam Pearl DeVere overdosed on morphine after one of the all night parties she liked to throw; and Mattie Silks' House of Mirrors in Denver, Colorado.

In 1901, May Palmer arrived in El Paso on vacation and planning to attend the Midwinter Carnival and look over possible new prospects in the frontier town. At the time, Palmer had a brothel in Tucson, Arizona that she had leased to another madam while she explored her options in Texas.

She bought an abandoned building at 309 Utah Street and was soon involved in completely renovating and outfitting the building that would eventually cost her $10,000. The new establishment was named Madam Palmer's Gentleman's Club and was soon staffed with twelve of the most attractive and exotic women Palmer could find.

Madams who ran the higher classed parlor houses often made up elaborate stories about their pasts, in order to entice customers as well as hide their true identities. Palmer refused to talk about her past and concentrated on making the Gentleman's Club one of the best and most fashionable parlor houses in the Southwest.

Madam Palmer's real name was probably Mary Elizabeth Eisenmenger. She was born in southern Illinois circa 1867. It is not certain if she gained a formal education or educated herself later, but Madam Palmer always used the best manners and grammar. Details of Palmer's early life are uncertain and those researching her history believe she drifted into prostitution, had a good business sense and soon started making money off her trade, plus she had a good reputation for treating the girls well who worked for her.

Pete Adams arrived in El Paso in 1893 to work as the assistant to the custom's collector. He had an outgoing personality, was reported to have been tall and handsome, and was quickly becoming known as the most eligible bachelor in town. He was also a favorite among the society women looking for a husband for their daughters.

Three years later, Adams quit his customs position and began dealing in wholesale liquor and soon opened his own saloon in the tenderloin district where Palmer had her Gentleman's Club. The couple would live together off and on for seven years before marrying and remaining together for the remainder of Mary's life.

During this time, Adams was put on trial by the local Elks' Club for being the husband of a prostitute and was later asked to resign from the organization. Possibly because of this, Palmer retired from her life as a madam in 1910 and according to most reports became a model housewife.

Madam Palmer loved wearing large, plume hats and was known for having one of the most extensive collections of them in the Southwest. She never left her residence without being adorned in one of her beloved hats. Palmer was diagnosed with cancer and passed away in Hot Springs, Arkansas in 1918 when she was fifty-one years old. Her husband Pete Adams was left with her estate.

Palmer's Gentleman's Club was elegant in every way. She even had gold-lettered, pressed tin signs made to adorn the door to her parlor house and for all twelve rooms belonging to the girls.

In H. Frost's book *The Gentleman's Club the story of Prostitution in El Paso,* he included a description of the parlor house and girls, "Palmer's girls would come into the parlor dressed in the most beautiful nightgowns, and wearing flowers in their hair. The girls got ten dollars a trick, which was a lot of money in those days, but it was cheap, considering the quality of the ladies."

The Gentleman's Club was not only elegantly adorned with brocade cushions, stuffed chairs, flowery carpets and period art work but also featured professionally done photographs of the girls who worked at the house or had in the past. Oval nudes hung in the stairwell and bedrooms of Palmer's establishment. These nudes were considered risqué for the respectable element of the time, but were eagerly sought in later years by those collecting western memorabilia.

***

Madam Pearl Devere's Old Homestead House in Cripple Creek, Colorado has received the distinction of being the finest parlor house in Colorado. Its front rooms were graced by mirrors, expensive furniture, oriental carpets, exotic wallpaper and a well-stocked liquor cabinet.

Old Homestead House — Cripple Creek, Colorado
Photo — Author's Collection

Pearl has been described as a beautiful outgoing woman eager to have a good time at a party. Like other madams of high class parlor houses she only hired the most beautiful girls she could find. Most of her girls had blonde hair, blue eyes, large bosoms, narrow waists and large hips, most of them weighed between 170 and 200 pounds.

Pearl often dressed in an outlandish manner even for sporting girls of her time, as she loved to be the center of attention and life of the party. She was infamous for throwing extravagant and wild parties lasting until the early hours of the morning. After one of these parties, Pearl was found dead lying next to one of her girls in 1897. It was later discovered she had taken an overdose of morphine. She was buried in an eight hundred dollar dress and given an expensive and well-attended funeral. The flamboyant madam's funeral was followed by a parade and celebration of her life while her friends and girls frolicked into the night, as their departed madam would have wanted them to do.

In 1895, Madam DeVere married a businessman named C.B. Flynn. It came as a surprise to those living in the red-light district, although Pearl continued her life much as she had before her marriage. Unfortunately, one afternoon a fire broke out and before it could be stopped had destroyed DeVere's house of prostitution and her husband's mill.

Flynn landed a job in Mexico smelting metal, which he sought in order to recoup the money they had lost in the fire. Pearl decided to remain in Cripple Creek and build her infamous parlor house the Old Homestead House. She had wallpaper imported from France at a cost of $143.00 a roll.

The Old Homestead House had running water and electricity during an era when most of the American public did not have these conveniences. Her establishment had two phones and an intercom system. Admittance to Pearl's parlor house was two hundred dollars a night when most rooms for those traveling were $3.00 a night.

Little has been discovered of Pearl's early life. She was known as Mrs. Isabella Martin when she first entered the trade, and it is believed she may have grown up in Indiana. Some sources point to the start of her career as a soiled dove when she took up with an infamous gambler named Billy Duetsch.

Duetsch is said to have broken the bank at Monte Carlo in Paris. During this time, he was known as a successful gambler. He may have encouraged DeVere to take up prostitution or it may have been her decision, but she would soon branch out on her own and become one of the most successful and infamous madams during the Victorian Era on the American frontier.

The Old Homestead House was converted into a museum in 1958 featuring stories and artifacts that bring the era to life.

***

Fannie Porter is described as a well-dressed, compassionate madam who was known for her discreetness when dealing with outlaw gangs frequenting her high-class parlor house on San Saba Street in San Antonio, Texas. She was especially loyal to Butch Cassidy, the Sundance Kid and members of their gang.

Fannie Porter's Boarding House is remembered as one of the most fashionable of its era with crystal chandeliers, colorful carpets and chilled champagne upon request. The boarding house was also known for its fine dining, four-post beds and satin sheets. She built her two-story house in 1883, and it soon became one of the more popular on the American frontier.

Porter appeared to be sincerely concerned about the girls who worked for her and even encouraged relationships with men outside the parlor house business. If she lost a girl in this manner, she was known to throw a wedding celebration. She paid for it herself and wished them well.

Four of the girls who worked for Porter became romantically involved with members of the Hole-in-the-Wall Gang and probably rode with them on some of their heists. These ladies of the night might have become famous because of their interaction with this infamous gang. The ladies were Etta Place, Lillie David, Maud Walker and Laura Bullion who are all believed to have worked at Fannie's boarding house during the years when the gang used it as one of their headquarters.

Madam Porter was frequently questioned by law enforcement about the whereabouts of the gang, yet she never revealed any information about them or the girls who had once been employees of her parlor house. Some sources state she kept in touch with the girls who worked for her for years afterwards. The girls thought well of her as she had a policy that if any of her girls were abused by a man, he would be forever banned from the establishment.

Porter was probably born in England and relocated to Texas when she was a year old. It is uncertain how she arrived in the United States and with whom, as there is no surviving information concerning the identities of her parents and siblings. She is first mentioned in the history of the area because of her relationship with Butch Cassidy and the Sundance Kid.

Some sources claim Porter was a young widow when she first became a prostitute, while others say she had her own parlor house in her early twenties. There is no question that Fannie Porter did exist, but with most shady ladies, the facts of her life and past are never verifiable.

The last known visit from Butch Cassidy and his gang to Fannie's Boarding House was in 1901. They had decided to split up and go their own ways. Butch, Sundance and Etta Place were planning to sail to Argentina and set up their own cattle ranch, where they hoped to go straight and live out their lives.

Fannie threw a huge going-away party for the gang. Unfortunately, while at Porter's they decided to have a group picture taken of the core members of the gang, and it would soon be posted on wanted posters throughout the country, an aid to the Pinkerton Detectives, investigating them who did not know what they looked like until the picture surfaced.

Wild Bunch Photo that became a Wanted Poster Photo — Author's Collection

No one is certain when Porter passed away, as after this 1901 party with the Hole-in-the-Wall Gang she fades from the pages of history books. There is no doubt she was a shrewd business woman who knew how to run a first-class parlor house. Some say she died in 1912, others have the date in 1949 in an automobile accident, but so far there is no real substantiated evidence as to when and where Fannie Porter died or spent the final years of her life.

Porter was mentioned off and on in the *San Antonio City Directory* between 1880 and 1902. She was listed as the head of the household and had five younger women living there. Boarding House was a popular term for these establishments during this era. She was ahead of her time in many ways, because she insisted her girls have good hygiene at all times. The women were also sent to a local doctor to insure they were disease-free for those gentlemen frequenting their establishment. Her parlor house had a good reputation and low crime rate.

Porter always let the women know that it was time to begin work with the following phrase, "There are gentlemen in the parlor ladies."

***

Mattie Silks' House of Mirrors was built by a popular madam named Jennie Rogers, who developed its reputation as a high-class parlor house. Upon Rogers' death, Silks bought the business and expanded it into the most popular house in Colorado during its time.

The house was perfect for Silks' taste with an elegant reception room and parlor with plate-glass mirrors covering the walls. A huge chandelier hung from the ceiling with hundreds of prisms sparkling upon brocade chairs and oriental rugs. There were twenty elegant bedrooms upstairs where gentlemen were entertained.

Legend says that Mattie was born on a Kansas farm in 1846 where she had no interest in the conventional life her family had planned for her. From a young age, Mattie wanted to run a fancy parlor house. It was her ambition since childhood and apparently her parents were not able to dissuade her.

By the time she was nineteen in 1865 she was running a small, parlor house in Illinois, and she may have been one of the youngest madams on the frontier. A story is told that her career was financed by a wealthy, Kansas City madam. She was in Denver, Colorado in 1876, where she remained for the rest of her career as a madam.

Madam Silks was described as a petite madam with a clear and creamy complexion, with blue eyes and blonde curls. She was always dressed in the latest and most expensive fashions and all of her clothes were made by the best tailors available. She also asked her tailor to conceal two pockets in the dresses she had made; in which she could carry her ivory handled pistol and the other for gold coins she might need.

Mattie was married twice and passed away in 1929 at the age of 83. Only four thousand dollars remained of the fortune she had made during her career as Madame Mattie Silks of the distinguished sporting house known as the House of Mirrors.

***

A history of madams on America's frontier would not be complete without mentioning a New Mexico madam named Sadie Orchard. She was not only a successful brothel owner in the mining towns of Kingston and Hillsboro in New Mexico's Black Range Mountains, but she was the state's first woman stagecoach driver. She possessed a quick business sense and at one time ran a restaurant and brothel in Hillsboro and another in Kingston.

She first arrived in the Black Range in 1886 where she set up a house of prostitution in Kingston. She claimed she had traveled from London's Lime House District where she learned about the life of a prostitute. For the remainder of her days, she touted a cockney accent and often used profanity and colorful language.

It was later discovered that Sadie, like so many working prostitutes during this era, had made up the story about her childhood and life before arriving in the Black Range. She actually grew up on an Iowa farm. Sadie was born in 1859 in Mills County, Iowa and was the fifth child of eight belonging to Bennett and Nancy Creech.

Her father fought in the American Civil War, and those years were as difficult for her family as they were to others living in the United States. Sadie's mother passed away when she was fourteen years old, and she soon assumed the responsibility and management of the family.

No one knows when Sadie first became a prostitute. Some sources hint that she was an actress before becoming a lady of the night. This could be where she learned to perfect her cockney accent.

The Creech farm bordered the land of a family from England. They raised horses, and Sadie may have learned her horsemanship skills as well as the cockney accent during these early years. Most madams cultivated as much mystery as possible about their identities and pasts.

Upon her arrival in Kingston, Sadie took on the dress and customs of the aristocratic British upper class. She, as most madams, dressed in the finest fashions of the era. Plumed hats were always a part of her attire.

As most madams were inclined to do in the interest of maximizing the business, Sadie only hired the most attractive women with vivacious personalities, and insisted they wear the latest fashions during working hours. When Sadie and her girls realized there was only one church in Kingston, they went to the saloons and local businesses asking for donations. They were able to raise $1500 and built a small, stone church for those wishing to attend services in the rugged, mining community.

When silver was devalued in 1893, Sadie decided to move nine miles down the road to Hillsboro. A couple years later she married Henry Orchard and they ran a stage line between Lake Valley and Kingston, with an overnight stop in Hillsboro. Sadie became the first woman stagecoach driver in New Mexico Territory.

Henry and Sadie had problems from the beginning of their rocky marriage. Henry had a great fondness for whiskey and could not resist drinking it whenever it was available. He also drank of the liquor supply Sadie had on hand for the brothel and restaurant. Sadie began to feel her husband's drinking was cutting more and more into her profits.

She ran Henry off more than once, but he always came back and she always let him. She even peppered him with a double-barreled shotgun one night, when she says she thought she was shooting over his head. He had her arrested for assault with a deadly weapon with intent to kill, and later she had him arrested for the same thing. The charges were always dropped.

The Orchards called their stagecoach line the Mountain Pride. It consisted of a concord coach and freight wagon. The operation had sixty-five mules and horses. It was most likely that Orchard had the mail contract when he and Sadie first met, but in later years she claimed she was the one who acquired the mail contract. The line was in operation between 1878 and 1882.

The stage line was also made up of six smaller passenger coaches for a charter service, as well as a mud wagon and other miscellaneous equipment needed to maintain the line. Those employed by the stage line hauled feed and water to different supply depots between Lake Valley and Kingston and maintained the extensive livestock herd needed for the operation. By 1900, the mines in the area were in decline and the boom was over resulting in a drop in demand. Miners were leaving the area everyday for new boom towns further sealing the fate of the communities in the Black Range.

In 1902, Orchard lost the bid on the mail contract, and soon the couple's stagecoach business starting losing momentum. Henry and Sadie divorced, but he remained in the area a few more years. He was often referred to as a common drunk. He later relocated to Belen in central New Mexico and then California.

Sadie's stagecoach has survived and is exhibited at the old, Murphy and Dolan Mercantile Store in Lincoln. A sign attached to the stagecoach tells Sadie's story as a tribute to her early years. There are currently no museums in Hillsboro or Kingston that could house the stagecoach, so it will remain in Lincoln.

Sadie had a reputation for having a salty mouth but otherwise people thought of her as a good, caring woman who was willing to lend a hand when needed. She often staked miners when they first arrived in the mountains and loaned money to merchants when they could not pay their utility bills.

Sadie's Ocean Grove Restaurant was a success, not only because of the girls waiting in the back rooms, but because of an exceptional Chinese cook Sadie hired to run her kitchen. Tom Ying immigrated to San Francisco from China and later ended up in Lake Valley where he owned a popular restaurant. Sadie was able to convince him to work for her in Hillsboro.

Ying had a temper, but he was accepted and liked by the community. He had a reputation for being honest and was said to never cheat anyone. Those who knew him said he enjoyed reading Chinese newspapers that came once a month, and he was also a great story teller.

Sadie passed away on April 3, 1943 in her beloved Hillsboro, but for unknown reasons was buried in Truth or Consequences. Her grave was neglected for a number of years until the Geronimo Springs Museum staff began to take care of it and to initiate the preservation of Sadie's intriguing history.

***

All of these elite parlor houses normally had a bouncer, servants and a professor. The professor's main duty was to supply music during the evening hours and while the ladies were relaxing after hours. He only earned a small wage but he was also paid in tips and whiskey. Different professors showed up every month, as they too traveled a circuit of parlor houses where they offered their services every few weeks or months.

The women working in the better establishments were never referred to as whores or prostitutes while gentlemen were in their presence. They were referred to as boarders and during their free hours they read books, did fancy needlework or worked in the garden.

The fancy madams advertised in many ways, but it seems two of the best methods were to send out fancy, engraved invitations or to advertise in a blue book directory found in the elite saloons, hotels and restaurants of large cities and settlements.

The first blue book appeared in New Orleans and was called *The Blue Book: A Gentleman's Guide to New Orleans.* It contained names, addresses and brief descriptions of different parlor houses, their madams and the girls who worked there. The practice would quickly spread describing classy establishments throughout the American frontier.

These classy establishments are all gone now. Many were torn down while others became apartment houses that fell into disuse in their later years. The distinctive and independent madams who founded the lavish houses of ill repute belong to the pages of history books.

The rip-roaring American frontier of previous years was on its way to being tamed by the time the railroad had traversed the country in the 1890s. The buffalo were all gone, as were most of the Native Americans who had hunted them. The cattle drives and military expeditions were in the past. The trails heading west were no longer full of homesteaders and pioneers trying to tame the land, as most of the available land had already been claimed.

A few reminders of the heyday of the Wild West remain. Abandoned buildings once housing stage stops, brothels, hotels and saloons can still be found. During this era, there was a steady supply of customers who met soiled doves and their madams in fancy houses where they could enjoy one another's company for a few hours.

These early soiled doves or ladies of the night were responsible for helping to open and settle the American West. They too headed west to make their fortunes and had enough ambition to try for something different than women of their era had ever experienced before or since. Their contributions to the history of the United States are much more significant than had previously been thought by earlier writers and researchers.

Chapter Two – Cowgirls, Wild West, Vaudeville & Rodeo Performers

Women first participated in rodeo events in the 1880s at local ranch rodeos and later as performers in Wild West shows and vaudeville acts in major cities throughout the United States. Buffalo Bill Cody was the first showman to give women a chance, and they soon became one of his most popular spectator events. These early cowgirls were often flamboyant, outgoing women who awed and intrigued their audiences.

The first female Wild West star was a lady sharpshooter who went by the stage name of Annie Oakley. She never rode broncs or performed tricks on the back of a running horse, but she would open the way for women with her sharpshooting skills. She was so popular that Buffalo Bill Cody decided to hire more women with varying acts and performance skills to join his Wild West show.

Oakley's birth name was Phoebe Ann Mosey and she grew up on a farm in Ohio. Her Quaker parents had nine children and Annie was the sixth. She lived a life of poverty during her childhood, as her father had passed away leaving her mother to raise the children on her own. Annie started trapping at the age of seven in order to procure food for the family. She was shooting and hunting a year later and sold the extra meat to shops in Greenville. By the time she was fifteen years old she had paid off the mortgage on her mother's farm, helping the family survive.

Annie would meet her future husband Frank Butler on Thanksgiving Day in 1875 when she attended a performance of the Baughman & Butler Shooting Act held in Cincinnati. Butler placed a $100.00 bet that he could beat any fancy female shooter. A shooting contest was arranged between fifteen-year-old Annie and Butler. The shooters were evenly matched, but Annie was able to win after Butler missed his 25th shot. The couple soon started to court and the following year they were married in August of 1876.

Annie and Frank began performing together and were offered a job with the Buffalo Bill Cody Wild West Show in 1885. Annie was only five feet tall and soon was given the nickname of Little Sure Shot. She and Frank traveled to Europe with the show and most historians agree that Annie was paid more than anyone else in Buffalo Bill's Wild West Show.

Annie, not only performed with the Wild West show, but she also felt it was her duty to teach other women to learn how to shoot and become comfortable carrying a gun. Some sources state she taught as many as 15,000 women how to shoot throughout her long career. She felt women needed a gun for protection and should know how to handle their guns in the same way they held their babies.

In 1912, the Butlers retired, bought land and built a nice house near Cambridge, Maryland. They lived in hotels while the construction of their home was underway. The house would become known as the Annie Oakley House and was listed on the National Register of Historic Places in 1996.

In 1917, the Butlers decided to return to public life. Annie had not lost her skill as a sharpshooter and continued to win competitions into her sixties. She passed away at the age of sixty-six in Greenville, Ohio in November of 1926. She and Frank Butler were married for over fifty years. The National Annie Oakley Center in Greenville, Ohio has an impressive collection of Oakley's personal possessions and memorabilia; as well as, her firearms are all on a permanent display at the center.

Annie was not afraid to pursue a career in which men had always excelled in the past. She also supported women's suffrage and believed women should have more rights. She and Frank performed together to large audiences throughout the United States and Europe for most of their married life.

Annie Oakley
Photo Author's Collection

Phineas Taylor Barnum of the Barnum & Bailey Circus would be the first to see the potential of having performers utilize the Old West in a Wild West show. At least forty years before Buffalo Bill Cody became famous for the creation of the rodeo and Wild West show, Phineas Barnum realized the untapped show biz potential when he bought a small herd of buffalo at a celebration at the site of the Battle of Bunker Hill near Boston.

While at this celebration, Barnum peeked inside an old, canvas tent and discovered a herd of fifteen young buffalo, which he immediately bought for seven hundred dollars. He shipped them to New York City and then had them transported to a barn near Hoboken, New Jersey. His circus soon added a spectator event called the *Great Buffalo Hunt,* and the New Yorkers who first saw the act went wild. Barnum presided over the first performance in New York City featuring a band of Indians from Iowa and his fifteen buffalo.

Another avenue many of these early rodeo stars took was performing in vaudeville during the off season of the rodeo circuit. Vaudeville was the most popular from the early 1880s into the 1930s. It is best described as a group of separate, unrelated acts grouped together in one show. There were singers, dancers, comedians, one-act plays, magicians, jugglers, minstrel shows, silent movies and more. Vaudeville has always been thought of as a variety, type show. Vaudeville first began to appear in saloons, freak shows and dime museums.

There were many types of entertainment available during these years, such as medicine shows that offered entertainment as well as tonics, salves and miracle cures. Eventually the Wild West show would evolve from these beginnings and incorporate many vaudeville acts into their program. There were several famous vaudeville stars whose names are still known today. W.C. Fields, Mae West, the Marx Brothers, Jimmy Durante, Jack Benny, Abbott and Costello, Bob Hope, Judy Garland, Sammy Davis, Jr., Red Skelton and the Three Stooges were all vaudeville actors.

Rodeo Cowgirls in the 1920s
Post Card – Author's Collection

A few of the first lady cowgirls were: Annie Shaffer, who was the first woman to ride a bronc at Fort Smith, Arkansas in 1896; Prairie Rose Henderson is credited with winning the first Cheyenne Frontier Days horse race for women in 1889; and Bertha Blanchett rode the first bronc at the Cheyenne Frontier Days Rodeo in either 1904 or 1905.

By 1920 most of the larger rodeos including the Cheyenne Frontier Days, the Pendleton Roundup, the Madison Square Garden Rodeo and the Calgary Stampede featured three women's events: bronc riding, trick riding and relay racing. Although, bronc riding was one of the first events where women excelled, by the 1940s it had been cut from the women's event list and it has never returned except at all-girl rodeos.

Women often sought the rankest bronc they could find in order to make a name for themselves. Women's bronc riding was extremely popular with the American public during the years it was a spectator sport. Among the reasons that led to its demise was there were more women killed riding broncs than men, rodeos were cutting back due to the shortages precipitated by World War I and rodeo for women was developing into a whole new profession.

Relay races remained a popular event for women rodeo stars. The biggest rodeos had large tracks, but not all of the smaller rodeo grounds throughout the country could afford to build these enormous tracks. It was common for relay racing to be conducted on dirt tracks near the rodeo grounds. The 1920s and thirties were the heyday of the relay racing events performed by women.

Most rodeo contests first began as part of a county fair or holiday festival, most frequently during the Fourth of July. The beginnings of the professional rodeo can be traced to Buffalo Bill Cody's first Fourth of July Celebration in North Platte, Nebraska in 1882. Cody was extremely popular because of his career as a buffalo hunter, vaudeville actor and dime store novel hero. Most Americans had heard about his exploits and wanted to see him in person. Buffalo Bill took his show on the road in 1883. The first Cheyenne Frontier Days Rodeo was held in 1897 and soon it became one of the premiere rodeos in North America. Buffalo Bill Cody took his Wild West show as far away as Europe and received excellent reviews and standing ovations everywhere he went.

Buffalo Bill Cody
Photo--Author's Collection

Wild West shows began to flourish on the frontier in the 1920s. Shows led by Pawnee Bill and Buckskin Hoyt, the Miller's 101 Ranch Wild West show and others provided entertainment at fairs and rodeos throughout the country. There were countless smaller shows that also toured the United States performing on Indian Reservations and in small towns.

Ruby — the Smallest Cowgirl
Photo--Author's Collection

One show was named Indian Pete's Wild West Show and originated in South Dakota near the Standing Rock Sioux Indian Reservation. He was also part owner of the Irwin Brothers Cheyenne Frontier Days Wild West Show and owned a cattle ranch near Lemmon, South Dakota. His show toured the country for a decade between 1910 and 1920. His entire family participated in the Wild West show events. His youngest daughter Ruby was often promoted as the smallest cowgirl, as shown in her publicity photo of that era.

Indian Pete's Wild West Show consisted of one band wagon, one ticket wagon, two chariots and a number of heavy baggage and pole wagons. He had agreed to pay for the wagons by the end of his first season in the Wild West show business. The wagons were later confiscated by a Minnesota sheriff's department when he had not paid the first installment fees he had agreed to pay. He claimed they had not made enough money to support the show yet as the business had been very poor along the route the show had chosen. In one Minnesota town they were actually forced to beg for food at private residences or they would have starved.

This shows the precarious existence of the smaller Wild West shows. They often had to provide a substantial amount of money when they first started their shows. They had to hire performers, buy animals and other equipment and food while the show traveled the circuit.

In the beginning, most cowgirls performing in both Wild West shows and rodeos wore simple floor-length divided skirts. These first female rodeo performers were often hindered by the clothes they had to wear, instead of wearing bloomers or jeans, they had to wear the cumbersome divided skirts and simple blouses of the era. Glenn R. Verman dates the invention of the divided skirt at 1902. This provides evidence that western women rode in a sidesaddle until after the turn of the twentieth century.

But, in the 1920s women began making their own elaborate costumes to wear during these performances. Prairie Rose Henderson, a Wyoming cowgirl has often been cited as being one of the most outrageous and daring of the cowgirls. Prairie Rose seemed to enjoy being a part of the rodeo circuit and training her animals to help with the daring stunts she performed.

Prairie Rose Henderson
Post Card --Author's Collection

She is listed in the National Cowgirl Hall of Fame, "Prairie
Rose Henderson made a name for herself during the golden
age of rodeo as a champion bronc rider. She became a fierce
relay racer, dazzling crowds not only with her daring feats but
also with her fashion sense and her flair for beautiful and
inventive costumes."

There are conflicting stories as to Prairie Rose's real name. She may have been from Ohio or Kansas but she spent most of her time when not performing at a ranch near Green River in southern Wyoming. She was one of the first women to participate in bronc riding. She questioned the judges at Cheyenne Frontier Days when they said she could not ride because she was a woman. When she forced the judges to review the rules, it was found there were no rules stating women could not ride and was allowed to ride at the event.

Prairie Rose definitely wins the award for most outgoing and flamboyant cowgirl of her era. She entered the Gordon, Nebraska rodeo wearing ostrich plumes over her bloomers and a blouse covered with colorful sequins. She enjoyed creating and making up her own costumes. Prairie Rose traveled to rodeo events throughout the United States and was a member of the Irwin Brothers Wild West Show by 1910. She was active in rodeos into the 1930s.

While residing on her ranch in Wyoming during the winter of 1932, Prairie Rose came up missing and although groups searched for her in the area, her body was not found for seven years. Her late husband was able to identify her body by a ring and championship rodeo belt buckle she was wearing. She had apparently lost her way during a fierce, Wyoming blizzard and froze to death. What an ending for one of the most famous and colorful cowgirls of the early Wild West shows and rodeos.

***

Lucille Mulhall is often credited with being America's first cowgirl. She was actually the first cowgirl to gain the undying admiration of the New York Press, and they nicknamed her the first cowgirl. Lucille was born in Missouri but when she was a child her family moved to a ranch near Guthrie, Oklahoma. She became an expert roper and bronc rider and her father Zack Mulhall ran her rodeo career; as well as, the careers of the rest of his children thereafter when they formed the Mulhall Family Wild West Show.

Lucille had her first public appearance at the 1897 St. Louis Fair and she was quickly on her way to a successful rodeo and Wild West career. The Mulhall family with Lucille as the star toured the country performing their rodeo skills to the delight of their fans. She performed for Teddy Roosevelt and was the most well-known cowgirl of her era especially after becoming a silent film star and dating Tom Mix.

In 1916, Lucille organized her own rodeo company called Lucille Malhall's Round-Up. Lucille would become the only female producer in the country and established new rodeos throughout the country offering employment and new competitions for women. During this era only one-third of all rodeo events were offered to women. Lucille loved to perform and even had several vaudeville acts before starting her own rodeo company.

***

Tillie Baldwin was another exceptional cowgirl during the golden years. Tillie immigrated to the United States from Norway and could not speak English when she first arrived. After watching some women Wild West performers practicing at a stable, she decided she too would like to support herself in that manner. She was eventually able to land a job trick riding with a man named Baldwin, and she took his last name as her stage name. By 1912, she was riding and performing for the infamous 101 Ranch Wild West Show and was popular with the public.

Tillie's rodeo costume is responsible for her success in many ways, as she was the first cowgirl to wear bloomers instead of the cumbersome divided skirt while performing. Her costume was much lighter than what other cowgirls were wearing and Tillie was able to easily perform her stunts. Many rodeo cowgirls of the era swore they would never wear bloomers but within a few years many were competing in the more comfortable costume. Many of the first cowgirls had fatal accidents due to the bulky, impractical floor-length divided skirts they were often required to wear. They were easily caught in the riggings causing fatalities and accidents.

Tillie Baldwin also became a champion at the sport of bull-dogging and was one of the first women to do so. It was one of the more dangerous sports in the rodeo, as women were expected to jump off the back of their running horse and land on the back of the calf to be bull-dogged. Tillie seemed to enjoy the sport and won most of the competitions of her era.

In 1919, Tillie returned to Norway and rode in the New England fair circuit where she gave exhibitions in bronc and trick riding plus bull-dogging. She married Wiliam Slate in 1935 but continued to ride in rodeos through the 1930s. When she retired from the rodeo circuit she spent many years as a riding instructor at a riding academy near where she lived in Connecticut. She passed away in 1950 at the age of seventy.

The arrival of World War I combined with the death of Buffalo Bill Cody in 1917 triggered a change in the way Americans felt about rodeo versus Wild West shows and vaudeville. For the first time in history, rodeos began to replace Wild West shows. The 1920s would be a time of extreme growth for the sport of rodeo and for the women who participated. Many Wild West shows began forming their own rodeo companies and developing the events as an athletic sport instead of a rodeo performance.

Tad Barnes Lucas was a famous trick and bronc rider and upcoming rodeo star of the 1920s. Lucas was born in Cody, Nebraska in 1902 and as most ranch kids she began riding horses at an early age. She also helped her brothers to break colts on the family ranch when she was seven years old. She along with her siblings took part in local rodeo contests and Wild West shows.

Tad moved to Texas with her brothers and started competing in rodeo events on a regular basis. She would soon go on to larger rodeos in Belle Fourche, South Dakota and Fort Worth, Texas. She became a full-time professional cowgirl starting in 1922. The next year, she toured the United States and Mexico with the 101 Ranch Wild West Show and took second place in the bronc riding at the Madison Square Garden Rodeo in New York City, one of the most coveted titles for lady bronc riders.

Lucas was invited to Tex Austin's London Rodeo and while in New York waiting for their passage to England she married a professional cowboy named Buck Lucas. Trick riding would take Tad to the top of her profession and she was one of the most well-known trick riders of her time. She had been fascinated with trick riding since she first discovered that she wanted to become a rodeo and Wild West star.

Tad Lucas was one of the most popular cowgirls during the 1920s and thirties. In 1923 Lucas took second place in bronc riding at the Madison Square Garden Rodeo and third place in the best-dressed competition. But, Lucas was hard to catch in the trick riding competition and won four titles in three years in Fort Worth, Boston and Philadelphia. She would go on to win two relay titles and two all-around titles in the mid-1920s. Although, she began her career in bronc riding, she was unable to win a bronc riding title until 1940 near the end of the era for lady bronc riders.

Even though the rodeo stars competed with one another in rodeo events, they also became good friends as they spent a lot of time together. In the early years of rodeo, there were no horse trailers, so their horses were often shipped by train to the next destination where they were going to compete. They often went in together to purchase an entire car on the train, because then they could ship all of their horses together at a reasonable rate. The cowgirls enjoyed these train rides, as they got to play cards, socialize and rest until their next event.

***

Eleanor McClintock Williams — Jim Williams Photo

Eleanor McClintock Williams was born to wealthy Pittsburgh artists in 1906, but left her luxurious and elite lifestyle behind to become a champion trick rider for Ringling Brothers Barnum & Bailey Circus and ride bucking horses in Tim McCoy's Wild West Show.

Eleanor was introduced to western life in the 1920s when on vacation at Nan Hart's Montana dude ranch. She became enthralled with horses and outdoor life. She decided to have her own dude ranch one day. She would begin a correspondence with Nan Hart that chronicled her career as a trick and bronc rider plus her purchase and development of the Rising Sun Dude Ranch in New Mexico.

In 1928, Eleanor attended a rodeo at Madison Square Garden and met her future husband a rodeo cowboy named Walter Heacock. Eleanor and Walter eloped two weeks later and joined a Wild West show bound for Chile. However, they were stranded when the manager ran off with the gate money. Eventually, they were able to find passage on a Japanese cargo ship and returned to the United States where they continued working the rodeo circuit.

A letter Eleanor wrote to her friend Nan Hart back in Montana explains how the trick and bronc riders traveled from one show to the next. She wrote, "We were traveling at a third class freight rate, and fully half of the time en route was spent sitting on the railroad sidings watching for regular trains to whizz by. We had no chair cars of any description, and the Ringling Brothers Pullman bunks are all built to stay put—they don't turn into seats by day."

Eleanor's first marriage did not last, and later she met a circus clown and they would marry and travel the rodeo circuit together. The couple joined Tim McCoy's Wild West Show in order to keep their dude ranch in New Mexico going. Tim McCoy would eventually go bankrupt because of this show. The show was supposed to surpass the 101 and Buffalo Bill Cody Shows. Riders came from everywhere: Argentina, Italy, Mexico, Australia, India, England and the United States.

Eleanor and her new husband decided to leave the show when she was injured during a performance. Her horse pulled away from the pickup man, then reared back hitting her in the face. The impact of the horse's head knocked her unconscious and drove one of her teeth through her upper lip cracking her cheekbone.

Eleanor writes about their return to New Mexico, "This was the first day of the Washington engagement, and I drew out what money I had coming to me that night, as did Earl, and we left the next day. And what a break for us that we did, as that was Monday, and Wednesday, creditors closed down on the luckless show and it went into the hand of receivers, and everyone got five dollars apiece."

Eleanor was inducted into the Cowgirl Hall of Fame in 1986 for her contributions to rodeo and western life. Her biography reads, "Eleanor's life epitomized that of the strong, independent western woman. She became a champion trick rider, performing on the rodeo circuit, Wild West shows and circuses. She purchased and built a ranch during the Depression, raised five children, ran for the NM Senate, was a published writer and became a recognized artist."

***

The first women bronc riders began to compete in rodeos in the United States at the turn of the twentieth century. For almost forty years, the women's rodeo event was one of the most popular on the rodeo and Wild West show circuit. Many of the early bronc riders grew up on ranches and helped to break and care for horses at a young age while other cowgirls had access to horses and knew how to handle them.

The 1920s was the heyday for lady bronc riders as audiences were enthralled by their horsemanship skills and exotic costumes and stunts. By, by 1933 with the deepening of the Great Depression, trick and trick roping were dropped as contest events at rodeos throughout the country. They became contract performers where they were paid for entertaining the audiences instead of competing with one another for the rodeo title.

At the end of the 1941 rodeo season ladies' bronc riding would be dropped from the traditional rodeo circuit. The Madison Square Garden Rodeo in New York City would be the first to drop women's bronc riding from their roster for the following year and premiere rodeos throughout the country would do the same. A few of the famous lady bronc riders continued to ride as an exhibition for another decade but the event has never returned to the traditional rodeo circuit.

Cowgirls who had ridden broncs were out of luck if they wanted to continue to ride professionally. But, in 1947 a few cowgirls got together and decided to start a ladies' rodeo association so they would be able to continue riding broncs, rope steers and even ride bulls if they wanted.

The first all-girl rodeo in the country was held in September of 1947 in Amarillo, Texas and the Girls Rodeo Association (GRA) was formed the following year. There were thirty-six all-girl rodeos held throughout the country in 1948 demonstrating the interest still held by the public in these rodeo cowgirls and their performances and competitions. In 1981, the name GRA was changed to Women's Professional Rodeo Association (WPRA). Each year the WPRA Finals Rodeo is held in Fort Worth, Texas in September.

Chapter Three — Lost Bird — From Wounded Knee, South Dakota

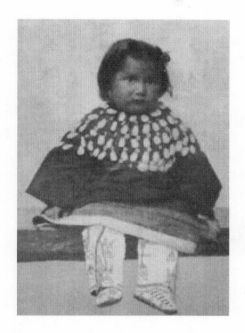

Lost Bird — Photo--Author's Collection

Note from author: The first time I learned about the massacre of Wounded Knee in Dakota Territory was in my Frontier History class in college. I was young and idealistic and could not believe the United States Cavalry would massacre over a hundred basically unarmed old men, women and children on a bitterly cold December morning on the South Dakota plains.

But, as I became a student of history I found the United States Cavalry was not always honorable in their dealings with Native American tribes they conquered on the American Frontier. They often resorted to killing women and children, massacred entire Indian villages while they were in their winter camps and nearly helpless, and seldom intended keeping any of the treaties they signed with these tribes.

Members of the Seventh Cavalry, possibly still wanting revenge after the Sioux and Cheyenne massacred Custer and his men at the Battle of the Little Bighorn in 1876, shot women and children as they ran for cover. The battlefield was littered with their frozen and bloody bodies. They would be carelessly thrown into a mass grave a few days later, many of the bodies still frozen in the grotesque positions in which they had died.

Decades before the Wounded Knee incident, the U.S. Cavalry under the command of U.S. Army Colonel John Chivington and two regiments of Colorado Cavalry units massacred a group of peaceful Cheyenne and Arapaho along the banks of Sand Creek in Colorado Territory in 1864. History has described the massacre as one of the worst atrocities against Native Americans committed during the Indian Wars.

Black Kettle and his eight hundred Southern Cheyenne had joined with an Arapaho band under the leadership of Chief Niwot to receive their provisions. They had been guaranteed safety and protection from the troops in the area. While they camped, many of their young men and the Dog Soldiers who protected the tribe had gone on a buffalo hunt.

The only people remaining in camp were the women, children and old men. Black Kettle even flew an American flag and a white flag underneath on his tepee to show the tribe was peaceful and did not want any problems. U.S. Army Colonel John Chivington and Colorado Cavalry units opened fire on the sleeping camp early on the morning of November 29.

Four years later in 1868, General George Armstrong Custer led another attack on a large group of Cheyenne camped along the Washita River in Oklahoma. They were another group of peaceful Indians camping on their designated reservation. Custer led a morning attack on the unsuspecting tribe killing mainly women and children. Chivington and Custer both were hailed as heroes after the massacres occurred.

I lived in the Black Hills region for thirteen years and was able to explore all the historic sites I had only been able to read about. I explored Devils Tower, Inyan Kara Mountain, Bear Butte, the Crazy Horse Monument and the site of Fort Phil Kearney, the Battlefield of the Little Bighorn where Custer was defeated; as well as, Mt. Rushmore, Deadwood, the Buffalo Bill Cody Museum, the Sturgis Motorcycle Museum, Custer State Park, Fort Laramie and Fort Robinson in nearby Nebraska where Crazy Horse was murdered. But, my visit to the Pine Ridge Indian Reservation and the battlefield at Wounded Knee left the most lasting impression upon me.

It was a warm, early summer afternoon and there was no one else around when I stopped and walked over the Wounded Knee Battlefield. It was extremely cold on the winter morning when the massacre occurred, and I had not yet experienced a winter on the Great Plains and did not realize how deadly they could be. The area was still wide-open rolling hills and it must have been easy for the cavalry with their superior military force to have easily overcome the fleeing Lakota.

I could imagine hearing the screams of the Lakota as they tried to save their families from the relentless gunfire and pursuit of the cavalrymen. I could picture them fleeing through the white and icy landscape while they attempted to protect their children and old people. From the reports I have read of the massacre, the cavalry was out of control and were so excited they shot their fellow soldiers. Once the killing began, the cavalry were unstoppable until they exterminated every Lakota they could find on the South Dakota plains that tragic morning in 1890. The ironic side of the story is that the Lakota were on their own reservation and were truly doing nothing wrong. If the cavalry had not over-reacted the story would have been much different, as would have been the ultimate outcome of the Indian Wars.

For most of the afternoon I walked through the battlefield with tears in my eyes and thought about that long ago December morning. My heart hurt for those who had lost their loved ones in such a cruel and senseless manner. I cringed as I imagined distant gunfire and the tragedy imposed upon the Lakota by the United States Cavalry.

To further add to their grief and humiliation, the Sioux were all thrown haphazardly into a mass grave after the soldiers had gone through their clothing and taken what they wanted for souvenirs. If no souvenirs were to be found, then they took fingers and other body parts. Not only did they massacre hundreds of innocent and undeserving people, but showed absolutely no respect for the dead. It is no wonder there were strained relations between Native Americans and the U.S. Cavalry.

***

On December 28, 1890 a detachment of the U.S. 7th Cavalry Regiment encountered a band of Miniconjou Lakota led by Spotted Tail en-route to the Pine Ridge Indian Reservation. The cavalry unit escorted the group of Native Americans a distance of five miles to Wounded Knee Creek where they decided to make camp for the evening.

The cavalry surrounded the group and the following morning started to disarm the Lakota. There are several versions as to what happened that day, but the following seems the most authentic. As the soldiers began to disarm the Lakota, an older man named Black Coyote did not want to give up his gun and a wrestling match ensued with the gun accidentally going off. That shot was the catalyst that drove the nervous cavalry members to open fire on the Lakota.

Many sources indicate that the cavalry went crazy and started shooting at women and children and even killed some of their own men in the frenzy. The Lakota were unable to keep up with the fire power of the cavalry and soon began evacuating their women and children. They fled, but the cavalry pursued them, killing anyone they saw moving including small children.

By the time the cavalry stopped, over one hundred and fifty Lakota were dead and another fifty wounded. There are other estimates that place the number of dead closer to 300, but the U.S. Cavalry naturally downplayed the number in later years when public sentiment turned against them. There is no doubt the Lakota were indiscriminately massacred that frigid December morning. The people were running away, hiding in ravines and trying to escape the deadly gunfire of members of the U.S. Cavalry.

Four days later, after more than one blizzard swept through the area, a burial detail heard the cries of an infant. After searching the area, they found a baby girl protected under the body of her mother who was frozen to the ground in her own blood. The child was frostbitten but alive. Her mother had her tightly wrapped for warmth and she was wearing a small, buckskin cap with beaded American flags on two sides.

Her Lakota relatives named her Lost Bird. In some ways, it might have been better if Lost Bird had suffered the same fate as her mother. Her relatives were not allowed to raise her, and she had a tragic life in many ways. She never felt accepted in the Native world or the white although she searched for her Lakota roots.

The discovery of Lost Bird soon came to the attention of Brigadier General Leonard Colby, who openly disobeyed orders and took Lost Bird into his household and adopted her. He never sincerely cared about her though, but thought of her more as a "curio" or a way to convince prominent Native American tribes to hire him as a lawyer or to advance his political aspirations.

But, his wife Clara Colby dearly loved Lost Bird and did her best to raise her. Unfortunately, she was busily caught up in the suffrage movement and did not always spend as much time with her daughter as she should. Leonard and Clara later divorced and the custody of Lost Bird remained with Clara.

Clara Colby worked with Susan B. Anthony and Elizabeth Cady Stanton, who are often attributed with being founding members of the suffrage movement. Colby was also a dedicated reformer in her own right and founded the *Women's Tribune* in Nebraska in 1883, and five years later it was the recognized newspaper of the National Woman Suffrage Association. Colby lived in Washington, D.C. half of the year so she could write about the suffrage movement's successes and upcoming events.

Neither of Lost Bird's adoptive parents had time for her, but they were the only parents she had ever known. They provided for her material needs but Lost Bird was often considered a curiosity amongst her parents' friends. It is not hard to imagine why Lost Bird became a difficult teenager and started to disobey her mother's rules.

Through the years, Clara placed Lost Bird in several different educational facilities, including boarding schools where she remained for most of the year. These experiences were often difficult for Lost Bird as she was not accepted by the other students. She was taunted about her Native American heritage and spent most of her time alone. Lost Bird began sneaking out at night and meeting boys and was not interested in receiving the education her mother Clara desired for her.

She wanted to return to South Dakota and learn about her people, so Clara placed her in a boarding school in Chamberlain, South Dakota where she did well and wanted to stay. But, when Clara changed her headquarters to a small town in Oregon, she decided to move Lost Bird to another boarding school for Native Americans in the area. Once again the other students made fun of her, and she was punished for wanting to know about the history of the Lakota.

She ran away from school several times before she was able to successfully get away. For some reason, she had come to suspect that she might be the daughter of Sitting Bull and wanted to find out if this was true (She was not the daughter of Sitting Bull). She left Oregon and made it as far as the tent city of Lemmon, South Dakota, about ten miles from the boundary of the Standing Rock Sioux Indian Reservation.

Since she was out of money she needed to search for work. She soon found employment with a man named Indian Pete Culbertson, owner of a newly organized Wild West show. One surviving story recounts that he was stolen from his parents while a child and raised among the Lakota, but then another claims he was an ex-con. Yet, not only did he run the Wild West show, but also had a large ranch near the reservation.

Indian Pete's wife usually rode in the show as a cowgirl, but she was pregnant in 1906 when Lost Bird showed up on the reservation, and she was hired to take the place of Indian Pete's wife in the show. Lost Bird seemed to take to the life of a rodeo performer and soon learned how to stand up on top of the saddle while the horse galloped at full speed. She also learned to vault off and on the horse, and then rode underneath the horse while holding onto the saddle.

Lost Bird dressed in broad-brimmed hats, colorful shirts and fringed leather skirts. She added a beaded bolero jacket, silk scarves, high boots and spurs with long, white fringed gloves. This type of western attire looked good on Lost Bird and she enjoyed her new profession. She quickly became a popular rodeo performer. But many people outside the show looked down on rodeo and Wild West stars and thought they were not quite respectable women.

With her brash personality and wild dress, the Lakota wanted to have nothing to do with Lost Bird. They thought she was too loud and demanding, and most thought she only claimed to be Sitting Bull's daughter as part of her act in the Wild West show. After awhile, she decided to move to California where Clara was living. If Lost Bird had approached her Lakota relatives in a more respectful manner, they could have answered all of her questions about her family lineage.

Lost Bird did not have good luck with men. She was married three times, and her first husband gave her syphilis and at the time there was no cure for the disease. She became extremely ill and was bedridden for a year while she recuperated and lived with Clara in Oregon.

Upon her recuperation, she decided to try for a career in acting and remain in California and for the time being decided to give up on finding her Lakota roots. She felt alienated amongst her people back in South Dakota. Lost Bird experienced a change in her luck and was hired by Pathe, an extremely successful producer of the era.

Cowboy and Indian movies were popular. Lost Bird appeared in several different movies including, the Round-Up, War on the Plains, Battle of the Red Men and the Lieutenant's Last Flight. She was perfect for the role she played as an Indian maiden on the plains.

By October of 1912 Lost Bird was destitute, but she thought her luck had changed when she met and married Bob Keith a cowboy from Texas. He had also arrived in California looking for film work, as he heard it paid cowboys $5.00 a day plus a free lunch to act in these films. The pay was much better than punching cows back in Texas.

Keith became a stunt rider, and his main skill was allowing himself to be dragged behind a running horse. Bob and Lost Bird were employed by the Pathe Film Company near Orange, California. The couple married in 1913 but Lost Bird soon found herself in an abusive relationship once more for when Bob was drunk he often beat her. She could not take Bob's abuse and before long left him.

Lost Bird decided to quit western films and landed a job with Buffalo Bill Cody's Wild West Show where she rode in the plains pageant. The show was merged with the Sells-Floto Circus for the 1914-15 Season and was an impressive extravaganza. The circus parade was over two miles long and consisted of 450 horses and 600 performers. There were two shows daily and the performance was always sold out, with much of the success owed to the name Buffalo Bill had made for himself.

Lost Bird met a circus clown with the performance named Dick Allen and the couple soon began seeing one another. He treated her better than her two previous husbands. They were both energetic and enjoyed performing in the show. Lost Bird felt the Wild West show and circus was the first real home she had ever had as she was appreciated and welcomed there.

After she and Allen married, they left the circus and joined a vaudeville troop that played dance halls, theaters and saloons in San Francisco's Barbary Coast. Dick Allen had a lariat-throwing act where he was quite proficient. The couple lived and worked in several different saloons in the red-light district. Unfortunately, there were already too many rope acts and Lost Bird was slowly losing her eyesight due to the syphilis. The couple finally gave up vaudeville and moved in with Dick's parents.

In February of 1920 Lost Bird became ill and passed during an influenza epidemic. Lost Bird's husband buried her in California, far from her South Dakota roots. Author Renee Sansom Flood researched Lost Bird's life and wrote the book *Lost Bird of Wounded Knee: Spirit of the Lakota,* a heart wrenching book that brought an awareness of Lost Bird's life and what she had lost by being taken from her people at such a young age. She never really belonged in either world.

Flood convinced the Lakota people to help her find and bring Lost Bird's remains to a cemetery near the battlefield at Wounded Knee, South Dakota. With the help of Flood and the Lakota, Lost Bird returned home to the South Dakota plains in 1991 over a hundred years after the massacre that forever changed her life.

Chapter Four--Molly Goodnight, Cornelia Adair & Susan McSween

Mary Ann "Molly" Goodnight lived a particularly unique life for a woman of her era. She was the first non-Native American woman to live in the Texas Panhandle before the Comanche were placed on the reservation and while the vast herds of buffalo still roamed the plains.

Molly grew up in a prominent family from Tennessee. Her father was attorney general of west Tennessee and a hero of the Battle of New Orleans. Her grandfather on her mother's side of the family was the first governor of Tennessee.

Her life would have been much different if her family had remained in Tennessee, but when Molly was fourteen years old in 1854, her parents decided to move to Texas. They moved their livestock and belongings in wagons and by boat to Fort Belknap in northern Texas. The fort was one in a chain of forts established to protect those settling the Texas frontier. The Dyer family was a large one with fourteen children.

Molly was a strong and resourceful woman, as demonstrated by her character when her parents passed away. Ten years after the family arrived in Texas, Molly's mother passed away and her father would follow a couple years later. Upon the death of her parents, Molly assumed the responsibility for her three youngest brothers: Leigh, Samuel and Walter. Leigh would later be hired as a drover for Charles Goodnight.

Molly assumed the care and education of her two youngest brothers. In order to support her family, Molly began teaching in a one-room schoolhouse in Young County. Charles first saw Molly when she arrived in the area escorted by a regiment of soldiers. Before long he was stopping at the schoolhouse to visit her. There were many young men interested in getting to know Molly, and Charles would court her for five years before they married.

Before their wedding in 1870, Molly with her two brothers traveled to Kentucky to visit relatives and prepare for the wedding. Charles and her bother Leigh went to Pueblo, Colorado first in order to start a new ranch before both traveled to Kentucky. The couple planned on moving to the ranch site after their wedding. Charles and Molly married in July of 1870 in her uncle's parlor in Hickman, Kentucky.

Returning to Colorado, the family traveled by boat as far as St. Louis, then by rail to Abilene, Kansas. From there they took a stagecoach to Pueblo, Colorado where they met friends at the Drover's Hotel before continuing on the final leg of their journey to the ranch. When they first arrived in Pueblo, there were two men hanging from a telegraph pole. Molly insisted that Charles move their ranch back to Texas.

Charles had a special wedding present made for Molly that she would use for the rest of her life; a custom-designed saddle. Women were constrained by the Victorian mores of the century and were expected to ride sidesaddle if they wanted to be considered respectable. Ladies' sidesaddles were dangerous and hard on both the horse and the rider but were the accepted way for women to travel on horseback. The saddle Charles had made for Molly was based on a man's regular saddletree with an adjustable side horn that curved downward instead of upward. In combination with the traditional adjustable stirrups, the individual could be better fitted, creating a more solid seat for safer riding.

Molly was an accomplished horsewoman and enjoyed riding the plains when she had time to do so. She often accompanied Charles on his cattle drives and enjoyed life on the trail. She rode with her husband on at least two cattle drives of over a hundred and fifty miles one way to Dodge City, Kansas, after the sale of the cattle they bought their first ranch.

The Goodnight family spent six years in Pueblo before returning to Texas and establishing the JA Ranch near Palo Duro Canyon. In 1876, Charles and his hands, including Leigh, Samuel and Walter, drove sixteen hundred head of cattle from Pueblo, Colorado to Palo Duro Canyon in the Texas Panhandle, where they staked a claim and established their "home ranch."

Charles had financial difficulties from the beginning and formed a partnership with John George Adair from Ireland. All Adair asked in exchange for his financial backing was that the ranch be named after him. The ranch was called the JA — short for John Adair.

On the Goodnight's first trip to the new ranch, they were accompanied by John Adair and his wife Cornelia. Cornelia Adair rode horse-back while Molly drove the wagon. The Adair's remained on the ranch for two weeks and then returned to Denver. Charles brought almost two thousand head of cattle with him on their first trip to Palo Duro.

Molly fell in love with Palo Duro Canyon and the endless plains surrounding it. Charles had built a log cabin for them at the bottom of the canyon. It was not an easy descent, as it was so steep that they had to take their wagons apart in order to make it to the bottom. It took them eight days to transport everything to the bottom. Next, the ranch hands constructed the buildings needed to complete the plans Charles had made for the ranch. Their first winter on the ranch was a "blizzard year" and many times Molly did not see the sun for days, but she often said these were some of the happiest times of her life.

Molly encountered the Kiowa and Comanche Indians who inhabited the area. One afternoon she found herself with unexpected guests at the ranch. The Comanche had been hunting buffalo on the ranch and when they found none, began killing Goodnight's cattle. When Charles discovered what they were doing, he invited the Comanche chief Quanah Parker to the ranch for a discussion. Goodnight and Parker came to an agreement that the Comanche could take two beeves every other day until they found buffalo, as long as they stayed out of ranch operations.

Molly was involved in every aspect of ranch life. She took care of the ranch business transactions and the cattle sale amounts. She often visited the line camps, taking along a small black bag that held her medical supplies. Since doctors were few and far between, Molly convinced her husband they needed a doctor in the area and he soon advertised for a doctor as she asked.

Molly and Charles had no children. So, Molly often mothered the cowboys employed on the ranch. She darned their socks and fixed them special meals, she would make a cobbler or pie and take it out to where they were working. She even taught them to read and write. To show their gratitude, the cowboys saved money and bought her a silver tea service so she could entertain in style when visitors came to the ranch.

Molly was interested in preserving the history of the ranch; as well as, learning the names of the plants and trees in the area. Yet, she was lonely at times living miles from the nearest town. Her only friends were three chickens given to her by an adoring cowboy. She and Charles were often seen riding together over the vast plains surrounding Palo Duro Canyon.

Charles and Molly built a major ranching enterprise on the Texas plains with the height of its productivity in 1885. There were nearly fifty houses on the ranch, dozens of large water tanks, many different corrals and two thousand bulls. It was one of the largest ranches in the history of Texas.

When Molly moved to the Texas Panhandle, the extinction of the buffalo was nearing completion. Normally, the buffalo calves were left to starve on the plains after the massacre of their parents. Molly could not bear to hear the cries of the starving buffalo calves while they remained near the dead, skinned bodies of their mothers. She was determined to save as many of the calves as she could.

One afternoon, she heard the repeated cries of animals in the distance. She decided to go and investigate and put them out of their misery if that is what they needed. But, upon finding the source of the lonely cries, she discovered two buffalo calves. She took them back to the ranch and they were the start of her buffalo herd that would become famous throughout the American West.

Molly began saving every buffalo calf she could find. She bottle fed them and before long Molly's buffalo herd had increased to nine hundred head. In later years, descendants of this original herd would help to establish herds in Yellowstone and Custer State Park in South Dakota.

Charles experimented with cross-breeding cattle and buffalo and soon was raising cattalo, a hardy breed of animal that could survive on the Texas plains. The herd would become known as the Charles Goodnight Herd, although it should have been more accurately named the Molly Goodnight Herd. Yet, Charles always credited his wife with saving the calves.

Molly was in her fifties by the time she and Charles moved to town. Although, she had loved ranch life she was ready to have more contact with people and civilization. Molly was instrumental in the founding of a junior college in Goodnight, and she was known as Aunt Molly to the college students before the institution was closed due to the opening of a teacher's college a few miles away.

Molly passed away on her beloved Texas plains in 1926. She left behind an important legacy of the history of the plains. Although, Molly and Charles often had financial problems, they did establish one of the largest cattle ranches in Texas history and tamed land that had been the home of the feared Comanche.

The JA Ranch, located southeast of Amarillo, is the oldest privately owned cattle ranch in the Texas Panhandle. At its peak, the ranch was comprised of 1,335,000 acres and spread through six Texas counties. The ranch was added to the National Register of Historic Places in 1966. Molly's husband, Charles Goodnight, was the first cattleman to bring herds of cattle onto the Llano Estacado on the southern plains of Texas, and discovered it was as perfect for sustaining large herds of cattle as it had been for the buffalo that had formerly roamed the plains.

Molly is credited with saving the buffalo from extinction as well as being an early conservationist. Living in such an isolated environment, she was afforded a certain freedom not available to all women during this era in United States history.

***

Buffalo Herd in Garden City, Kansas
Post Card --Author's Collection

The American bison is often associated with life on the last of America's frontier. Although, the bison became known as plains animals, this has not always been the case. At one time buffalo roamed between Canada and Mexico and from the Rocky Mountains to Kansas. Most wildlife biologists believe the bison traveled across the land bridge between Asia and Russia and migrated, as did Native American tribes, to escape the climatic changes forcing them to seek better conditions.

There were more than enough buffalo to supply the needs of the Native American tribes who resided on the Great Plains. They relied on the buffalo for food and clothing as well as shelter. They used every portion of the bison and were thankful to the animal for providing for their needs. Their lifestyle became entwined with the buffalo, and they believed their association with the animal was a spiritual partnership.

Before the arrival of the horse in the 1600s, the Native Americans used several different methods when hunting the buffalo. Hunting and procuring their winter meat supply was much more difficult without the horse and gun. Some tribes imitated wolves while wearing wolf skins and were able to get within shooting range with bows and arrows. The most successful method was the buffalo jump, where the tribes rushed the animals to their deaths over a cliff or into a ravine and then easily finished killing the injured bison.

***

Cornelia Adair had the heart of a rancher's wife, even though she was born to wealthy, prominent parents in Philadelphia and grew up among the socially elite. She would help her husband, along with Charles and Molly Goodnight, establish one of the largest and most successful cattle ranches in the history of the United States. The ranch was named the JA Ranch after John Adair, Cornelia's husband. After the death of John Adair, Cornelia would continue visiting the ranch and sending money for its upkeep and management.

Cornelia was born in 1837 to James Wadsworth, Sr. and the former Mary Craig Wharton. Her parents were pioneers in New York's Geneseo Valley in the 1700s. After first settling the land, they built magnificent estates and named them the Homestead and the Hartford House.

Cornelia's family often traveled and in 1855 they took an extensive trip to England and France. When they returned, Cornelia married Montgomery Ritchie of Boston. The couple would have two sons. Cornelia's husband and her father both passed away during the American Civil War. To escape her memories and recover from the pain of their deaths, she took her two sons overseas for an extensive tour of England and France.

A few years later, she returned to New York and attended a political ball at the home of Congressman J.C. Hughes and met her future husband, John Adair from Ireland. Adair had estates in Ireland and England and the couple often spent time at one or the other during the year. Both of the Adairs were eager to visit the American West and experience a cattle drive or a buffalo hunt before it was too late. John Adair, who had never cared for New York, decided to establish his business headquarters in Denver.

In the summer of 1877, the Adairs and Goodnights became partners in a ranching enterprise on the Texas Plains. Charles Goodnight located the ranch headquarters in Palo Duro Canyon, as he thought the location would provide excellent grazing for the cattle; as well as, protection from the winter blizzards commonly plaguing the area during the winter months.

Charles Goodnight would manage the ranch, while Adair provided the financing. The partnership was successful until Adair's death in 1885. At that time, Cornelia bought out the Goodnights and decided to hire her own ranch manager and become involved with the running of the ranch. Although, Cornelia continued to live at her late husband's estate in Ireland, she returned to the United States each fall. While visiting the ranch, she looked over the cattle and played an active role in administering John's estate, calculating her own profits and losses. In 1917, the ranch encompassed 500,000 acres and was stocked with 30,000 head of cattle and seven hundred horses.

Cornelia used her wealth to support many civic projects near the ranch headquarters. She is responsible for building a hospital in Clarendon, Texas; as well as, the local YMCA building where she also provided money when needed. She also helped support the local Episcopal Church and Boy Scout movement in both the United States and England. She was an extremely generous person and enjoyed spending her money to help organizations and those in need.

Cornelia left behind a fascinating diary written in the fall of 1874, when she and her husband John visited the United States in order to participate in a buffalo hunt, and at the same time explore the American West. She leaves a vivid description of her travels and experiences between the months of August and November.

It seemed everyone was hunting buffalo, not only to make a profit, but to be able to say they had killed one of the last buffalo on the plains. The local clergyman had not preached a sermon for five weeks because he was often hunting buffalo, while others planned on hunting for the winter. There was a fever among the people to get out and kill as many buffalo as they could before there were none left.

When Cornelia and John arrived on the Platte River, they would encounter many of the settlers who did not approve of the buffalo hunters and tried to keep them away. Cornelia stated in her diary, "There is great harm by buffalo hunters, as the buffalo meat is their principal support for the first few years."

The first day that the couple went hunting for buffalo was not as successful as they had hoped and they found few of the beasts. Eventually they thought they saw a larger herd of buffalo a few miles in the distance but upon approaching the herd, they found only black cattle. They saw herds of grazing antelope, wolves, many hawks and then more antelope. They could not locate a buffalo herd anywhere in the area. They even found a dead buffalo that had been shot by someone else weeks before.

By late afternoon, they came upon their first buffalo herd, described by Cornelia in her diary, "When we were on top of a hill, very distant little dark spots were seen moving: glasses instantly out. Buffalo? Yes, buffalo; more come up, a good herd; we galloped on, keeping as hidden as possible behind small ridges, until within a half-mile from them: they came in full view, some lying down, some with calves, we cantered towards them."

The buffalo did not pay much attention to the hunters at first, but as the riders approached, the bison started to gallop away from them. According to Cornelia's diary, it was too dusty to see everything that happened that day. Soon, John and others in the hunt tried to separate a buffalo or two from the group. She noticed they had been successful and rode in their direction to watch the process. When she got closer she saw a horse and rider were down and upon close inspection discovered it was her husband who was pinned under his dead horse. John's horse had not wanted to get too close to the buffalo and when Adair tried to urge him on his pistol had fired killing the horse. Amazingly, John was not seriously injured.

The hunt did not go as well as expected that day, as they found one of the soldiers on the ground where he had been upended from his horse. It seemed his spine had been injured and he was in considerate pain. Cornelia's husband John received a shoulder injury and it was difficult for him to ride the remainder of the day and participate in the buffalo hunt.

While trying to make their way back to camp, they encountered another herd of buffalo, but the luckless hunters only wanted to get some rest at this point. Cornelia describes how they felt upon returning to camp, "How tired we were! For a moment our spirits revived when, after washing off the dust and heat, we found a delicious thick soup of buffalo-meat awaiting us in the cheery mess-tent; but all felt more or less downhearted," she wrote.

Participating in the buffalo hunt seemed to cure the Adairs of their need to hunt buffalo on the Great Plains. Cornelia explained, "John's shoulder was so painful he could not move it, and shooting was at an end for him for several days at least," she wrote. "Our forage was exhausted and our horses could not run buffalo. So we decided to make for Sydney (Nebraska) as soon as we could. Rather an inglorious wind-up to an exciting day!"

***

Lincoln, New Mexico Circa 1920
Post Card -Author's Collection

Most people have heard of Billy the Kid, Pat Garrett, John Tunstall and New Mexico's Lincoln County War. Yet, Susan McSween, an important player in the history of Lincoln County has often been overlooked or only briefly mentioned in history books. She not only survived the death of her husband Alexander McSween and the burning of their home in Lincoln, but she went on to become a successful rancher and was nicknamed the Cattle Queen of New Mexico.

Susan Hummer was born in Adams County, Pennsylvania in 1845. She grew up in an extremely religious family belonging to the German Baptist sect known as the Brethren. The group believed agriculture was the only profession for devout Christians. As a child, Susan dressed in gray, black or blue frocks and a white apron and attended religious ceremonies throughout the week.

Susan had an unhappy childhood. Her mother passed away when she was a teenager and her father remarried a woman that was not always fair to his children. Susan's brothers and sisters left home as soon as they could. Susan's father had never been the affectionate type and normally sided with his new wife over his own children when conflicts occurred.

The Hummer family farm was near Gettysburg and during the Civil War the family had to take cover in the basement to avoid a stray bullet. Susan would leave home shortly after the battle in 1863 when she was seventeen years old mainly due to the cruel treatment of her stepmother and an uncaring father. Little is known about Susan's life for ten years until she married Alexander McSween in 1873.

The couple first met at the Perkins Hotel in Perkins, Illinois in 1870 and would start a three year courtship while Alex worked on his law degree and Susan took piano lessons at a convent nearby. In the beginning, they planned on building their future in Kansas and moved to Eureka after their wedding. They stayed in the local hotel while building their large, Victorian style home. Alex worked as a teacher while he completed his law degree and the building of their home.

When the Eureka Bank collapsed a few years later, the McSweens decided to move to a new location with a more stable economy. They sold as much of their property as they could but still left the state almost penniless. They had decided to settle near Silver City in New Mexico Territory. Alex hoped the arid climate would help his problems with asthma. The couple traveled southward with other families escaping bankruptcy and foreclosure in Kansas.

They traveled in a buggy pulled by horses and followed the Atchison, Topeka & Santa Fe Railroad line to their new home in New Mexico. They left Eureka in September hoping to avoid the rainy season. There were lots of people traveling in those days and the McSweens camped with others who were moving to the Southwest.

They met others along their route who said Lincoln was the up and coming town in New Mexico Territory, and the McSweens decided to make their home in Lincoln instead of Silver City. Spanish settlers had been living there for decades and named the location La Placita del Rio Bonito. The town of Lincoln was in desperate need of an attorney and Susan and Alex headed southeast in the direction of Lincoln and the fate that awaited them.

They were almost out of money when they arrived in New Mexico Territory. The road to Lincoln was not much more than wagon wheel ruts taking them across one hundred miles of cactus and sagebrush. The couple arrived in Lincoln in March of 1875.

The village of Lincoln was an impoverished looking community with a torreon in the middle where the settlers went to wait out Apache raids. They told of many a night when they had to remain inside the torreon for hours while the Apache screamed and rioted outside.

Torreon in Lincoln
Post Card--Author's Collection

The McSweens managed to find a boarding house where they lived while looking for a more permanent dwelling. They eventually located a small, crude cabin where they lived while looking for land and saving money to build their own house.

At the time the McSweens moved to Lincoln it was one of the most violent communities in the United States. The criminal and law enforcements elements both were corrupt and the gun ruled more than the law. Most of the people took the law into their own hands and settled their own problems. It was not unheard of to be shot in the back if you were on the wrong side of the two factions in control of Lincoln County.

Shortly after Alexander McSween opened an attorney's office in Lincoln, John Tunstall from England moved to the United States and settled on land near San Patricio where he prepared to go into the ranching business. He would also see the potential for a mercantile business in Lincoln as well, and this would upset the Murphy and Dolan faction as it took away from their profits.

McSween would build a nice, Victorian style house on Lincoln's Main Street to the west of the location of John Tunstall's mercantile store. The town newcomers to the area went about the business of settling into a new location and learning a new culture. But, from the beginning there were serious problems between the two factions.

It all came to a head one afternoon when John Tunstall was murdered while en-route to Lincoln. Billy the Kid and other ranch hands knew who the killers were and formed a group known as the Regulators and went after his killers. This would cause the Lincoln County War to explode with killings occurring on both sides.

Susan's husband was gunned down on the streets of Lincoln while trying to escape his burning home in 1878. She had financial difficulties in the years following his death. She received help from John Tunstall's family, and she served as the executor of his estate in New Mexico. Two years after her husband's death in 1880 she married another attorney named George Barber, although they would divorce a few years later.

John Chisum gave her a herd of forty cattle to start her in the cattle business. She established her cattle ranch near Three Rivers between Tularosa and Carrizozo and by 1890 she owned at least three thousand head of cattle. She planted extensive fruit orchards and became involved in mining. She owned land in White Oaks and Engle across the White Sands to the west. She was referred to as the Cattle Queen of New Mexico during these years.

In 1902 she sold her ranch near Three Rivers and lived in White Oaks full-time, a mining community to the north. Her final days were not so grand as she had to sell much of the exquisite jewelry she had accumulated over the years in order to cover her debts. She passed away at the age of 85 in 1931 and is buried in a cemetery near White Oaks.

Chapter Five – Lucille Mathews & Living South of the Border

Lucille Mathews Boyle Reynolds
Lucille Reynolds Photo

Lucille Mathews was born near the railroad town of Abo west of Mountainair in 1932. Dr. Amble, the local doctor made a house call to help with her birth. Lucille has lived the life of a genuine true pioneer woman. She camped out in a cave with her family in the Manzano Mountains while her father built the log cabin that would become their home and she rode horse-back to a one-room schoolhouse to receive an education. Her father, John Mathews, logged nearby in order to support the family during these years.

Lucille describes these early years, "By the time I attended school, we had built a log cabin in New Canyon on the road to Capilla Peak. I rode horse-back each day to the Union School three miles away," she pointed out. "The teacher lived in a cabin near the school. There was no electricity or running water and we used an outhouse when needing a bathroom break."

Everyone took their lunch to school in those days as this was before the era of school cafeterias. Lucille explained, "I carried my lunch in a bag mom made for me to hang around the saddle horn. My lunch was carried in a small lard bucket and I carried water in a pint jar."

Making a living was not always easy in the 1930s and forties throughout the United States. The Great Depression and coinciding dust bowl years made it difficult for farmers to survive. Many homesteaders left their farms and never returned while others moved elsewhere for a few years to find employment, returning to their farms when the drought years ended.

John was offered a job with the U.S. Department of Agriculture vaccinating cattle from Mexico against foot-and-mouth disease. The cattle were vaccinated and quarantined in Mexico to insure they could safely cross into the United States without spreading the disease. Lucille explained what John had to do to get the job, "Dad traveled to Las Cruces to New Mexico State University and passed all the examinations to work with the program, he had spoken fluent Spanish all of his life. The applicants were required to speak Spanish."

John left the family behind in January of 1949 and traveled to Mexico City where he would join others helping in the vaccination of the infected cattle. The family followed in April and settled at Guadalajara, near Mexico City and lived in the Hotel Palacio.

Hotel Palacio in Guadalajara where the Mathews' family lived in Mexico--Lucille Reynolds Photo

The family traveled to Guadalajara and back several times during their three year stint south of the border. They lived among the native people and made good friends while learning a new culture and language. They hated having to leave John behind when they returned to the states so Lucille and Barbara could attend school in Mountainair. Lucille explains, "Dad remained in Mexico. He drove us to El Paso and then flew back where he would use the truck assigned to him by the government for transportation and work," she said. "I drove the family the rest of the way home to Mountainair and we missed him during that drive home."

On one of their trips to Guadalajara they spent the night in Monterey in a lovely hotel but the plumbing did not work. According to Lucille, it took longer to travel across Mexico during these years, "There were no freeways in Mexico when we lived there, with only two lane roads although most of them were paved," she explained. "At 55 mph and two lane roads, it took a lot longer to make that trip than today. But in many ways, it was probably a lot safer to travel those roads than it is today too."

Lucille tells the story of what happened when they tried ordering a meal without knowing the language, "No one knew Spanish and there was not a thing listed on the menu in English. There was one man who knew English and offered to help us order. We ordered chicken fried steak. They brought us both chicken and fried steak. We ate the steak but took the chicken back to the hotel to eat later. Coca-Cola products were the same as in the United States, but they were always sold hot not refrigerated like back in the states."

Their final year in Mexico, Lucille decided to attend Eastern New Mexico University in Portales while the family returned to Mexico. Lucille has often said if she had it to do over, she would have gone to Mexico with the family instead of attending college. They were always a close-knit family and it was hard for her to remain behind in the United States without them.

The Mexican and United States Governments worked together between 1947 and 1952 to eradicate foot-and-mouth disease in Mexico. The first outbreak of the disease was reported on November 4, 1946 in a Veracruz newspaper where three hundred sick animals had been discovered and of that number twenty-five died. The cattle were affected by the disease to such an extent that there was a shortage of milk.

Don Stoops, assistant agricultural attaché at the United States Embassy in Mexico City wired officials in Washington about the reported outbreak. The United States soon sent American veterinarians to help in diagnosing the disease and closed the border between the two countries. It became illegal to move animals or animal or vegetable products across the United States and Mexican border.

When the disease was first noticed, the infected cattle were slaughtered and buried, but by the time John and the team from the United States arrived, the animals were being vaccinated against the disease. But, the Mexican people remained suspicious and often hid their cattle and shot at those who were trying to help them.

The Mexican people often moved their cattle off into the hills and hid them in caves or canyons so they would not be killed or vaccinated. Many times the military had to be called in to protect the group of American workers and they were required to carry guns. But, as the success of the program spread the cattle owners grew to trust the Americans but never completely. Some sources point to the infection originating with a group of bulls from Brazil, but whatever the cause it was a difficult and stressful time in Mexico's history.

Barbara, Opal & Dan in 1949
Lucille Reynolds Photo

Near the end of her first year in college, Lucille received an urgent phone call from John asking her to come to Guadalajara as soon as she could take her final exams. Opal, her mother had contracted malaria and she needed to help take care of Dan and Barbara, as well as attend her medical appointments. Lucille took her finals early, while her cousin Lorraine was preparing to fly from Seattle to Albuquerque so she and Lucille could make the trip together.

Lucille and Lorraine had done very little traveling alone up to this point in their lives, especially outside the United States. John gave his daughter the following instructions, "Relatives will take you and Lorraine to El Paso where you will get a room at the Del Norte Hotel and I will call you there. Then you will have to find your way to the Juarez Airport and catch the first plane to San Luis Potosi where I will be waiting for you."

The girls followed John's instructions and got on a plane in Juarez, Mexico. The plane stopped at every little town along the way, unloading and taking on passengers. It also gave them time to take a bathroom break, since there were no facilities on the plane. Both girls could speak a little Spanish and were also able to communicate with hand signals. Yet, they were relieved to see John and Dan waiting for them at the airport.

Later, the family moved to Tlajomulco, a town near Guadalajara where they made good friends and lived across a central courtyard from their neighbors. The family loved living in Mexico, as the people were friendly and accommodating. The living conditions were primitive, but the family had not been used to much better amenities back on the bean farm in New Mexico. They lived without electricity and carried their water from a well in the center of town. Their neighbors all knew and watched out for one another.

The family normally cooked for themselves, but also bought food at the open-air Mexican markets. Lucille explains how the meat was sold, "There were certain days of the week when meat was butchered down the street. During the evenings the taco makers set up their fires along the street where they also cooked corn on the cob." There was also a grocery store on the corner and a bakery down the street. The one food item Lucille missed the most was ice-cream, as during those years it could not be found in her Mexican village.

A bus traveled back and forth to Guadalajara each day. Not only did it carry passengers but bottles of water. Lucille explains, "We got drinking water from five gallon containers delivered by the bus driver." The streets where they lived were made of cobblestones; there was no pavement. Most of the villages had a Catholic Church and a school.

On Saturday nights everyone went to the plaza and listened to music and danced. Lucille attended the dances with her family and friends. The Mexicans had a custom where boys and girls would walk around the plaza in different directions. The boys would offer the girl of their choice a rose and if she accepted the flower had implicitly agreed to dance with him for the rest of the evening. Lucille was not aware of the tradition and had an armful of roses before she was informed of what she had agreed to do. She rushed home to avoid hurting anyone's feelings. Swimming and watching trains pass were also popular activities among the kids.

Kids Loading up to Visit the Train
Lucille Reynolds Photo

Lucille relates the story of how there had been a family feud that erupted into violence near a favorite swimming hole used by the town. There was blood along the path covered by palm leaves where someone had been murdered. Lucille's father John often remained on guard during these swimming excursions insuring the safety of the family.

All of the homes had bars on the windows in an effort to protect the women from abduction. One of the girls in the town had been taken and abused before family and friends were able to find her. Those living in the town were cautious and kept the children in sight at all times especially their daughters.

They were the only family in the village who were from the United States. Most of the people could not speak English and Opal and Lucille could speak little Spanish. Dan and Barbara, being young children soon picked up the Spanish language and could communicate freely with the other children.

While traveling throughout Mexico it was often difficult to find an eating establishment that was clean and sanitary. Lucille tells how they looked all over town for a place to eat and decided upon the bus station because they thought it would be cleaner than the other eating places. As they walked into the bus station a pig ran out the back door and flies were thick on the surface of everything, but the locals did not seem to notice or be bothered by them.

During their travels, they saw many colorful, wild parrots as well as exotic religious customs. They encountered Mexicans walking along a much, rutted trail to a little church. Many had cactus attached to their naked backs as they sought penitence during the Easter season. They were an extremely religious and devoted people, according to Lucille, who observed many of their ceremonies and traditions.

Lupe & her Daughters Mary & Lucy
Lucille Reynolds Photo

During the two years they lived in Tlajomulco, they leased an apartment with an adjoining courtyard from a Mexican woman named Lupe. Barbara and Dan became good friends with the neighborhood children and soon learned to speak the language fluently. The children often played together in the courtyard and Barbara relates a story in which the family barely avoided a tragedy.

"One night we were playing hide and go seek, and I hid between a pole that was a support for the ceiling of the patio and the well wall. Usually, the bucket was sat on the wall that was around the well, but for some reason whoever pulled up the water the last time, left the bucket dangling on the rope on the windlass. A windlass is a piece of equipment with two handles where two people could get on either side and wind up buckets of water," Barbara pointed out.

She goes on to describe what happened next, "All of a sudden, the bucket started to rapidly drop into the well, and the handles of the windlass started whirling over my head. It scared me, and when I jumped up to run, one of the handles hit my head a glancing blow and scalped me," Barbara explained. "I was immediately covered in blood, and in my young mind I thought my head was split."

One of the neighborhood ladies picked Barbara up and ran to the pickup truck nearby and soon the whole town was in an uproar. Young Barbara thought her head would split open and her brains would fall out if she didn't hold her head together, so she rode all the way to Guadalajara in that position.

When they arrived at the hospital, Barbara did not want them to put her to sleep because she was afraid she would never wake up. Opal convinced her she would be alright, "They allowed Mama to stand right there by my side while they put me to sleep, shaved my head and sewed me up. She said they raked my long hair out from under my scalp and shaved my head. Knowing Mama, it's a wonder she didn't pass out, but she didn't. She saw it all," Barbara stated.

Barbara was more upset about the penicillin shots she had to take than having a bald head while her hair grew back. She relates the reasons why, "The penicillin shots in those days were a thick serum that hurt like the dickens. My bald head bothered Mama more than it did me. She made me a little scarf to wear over my head, but it was a bother to me, so I just ran around bald-headed."

By the family's last summer in Mexico, John too had contracted malaria and the family decided to return to New Mexico. John and Opal returned in one vehicle with Lorraine and her father. Lucille, Barbara and a family friend packed the family's belongings and then returned in the family truck to the states after taking care of closing out the family's business in Mexico. They had many challenges along the way, especially when one of the tires blew out and the spare was not much better. They had to hobble into the nearest town and trade for a new one.

Instead of returning to college when the family returned to the states, Lucille worked at various jobs before meeting Robert Boyle, who was working on a road construction project that had recently arrived in Mountainair. They married and started raising a family and developing a cattle ranch.

She lived on the road with Robert (Bob) the first years of their marriage as he traveled from one road construction site to another, but they would eventually purchase land south of Mountainair where they started a small, herd of cattle that would become the family ranch. Lucille's son continues to run the ranch where she still lives.

Lucille went on to live an active, eventful life but has never forgotten her Mexican friends and treasures the memories they shared.

Lucille on Snooper in the 1950s
Lucille Reynolds Photo

Barbara Mathews in 1962
Photo--Author's Collection

Chapter Six – Pioneer Teachers & Their Contributions

Mabel Sibley Jones – Frontier Teacher
Photo--Author's Collection

Countless women left the comforts of home and family behind in order to open schools and provide educational opportunities for children throughout the American frontier. These first teachers often boarded-around (meaning they lived with a different family each week or month), taught in primitive conditions and encountered customs and traditions much different from what they had ever experienced before.

Up to the mid-nineteenth century, men were considered better at teaching than women and it was actually hard for them to find a job in the profession. Those women who were lucky enough to find a job in the field were often considered incompetent and unable to control a class of students. But, these thoughts would start to change shortly afterwards with the rising population inhabiting the frontier.

Much of the public opinion against women started to change in 1845 when a woman named Catherine Beecher published a booklet titled: *The Duty of American Women to their Country.* She proclaimed in her writing that it was the duty of women to head to the frontier and found schools and find teaching positions. If they did not do so the population increase would outgrow the teachers available. These children would grow up in ignorance unless women came forth to teach them.

Beecher was able to impress the importance of teaching on the frontier to a number of teachers in New England. Women outnumbered the men in this region of the country due to emigration and seafaring. Many of these women left behind wanted a new adventure for their lives and soon moved to the American frontier in order to fill teaching positions.

These first teachers from New England made an impression on their employers because by the late 1850s school systems were begging for women from New England to teach in frontier schools. Surprisingly, there were few requirements for these women schoolteachers. They were asked to give the school system a pledge that they would not get married for at least one year and it would be best if they remained single for three years. For some reason during this era in United States history women were not allowed to teach after they married.

Women had to possess a passion for teaching on the frontier as the conditions were primitive and lacking in the modern conveniences of the era. The average wage for teachers was $12.00 a month. There were many schools that paid by the head or one dollar per pupil per month. Board and lodging were provided by the families hiring the schoolteacher and she was expected to help out with the cleaning and cooking. It was not uncommon for these early teachers to change boarding places every two weeks, walk three to six miles to work no matter what was happening with the weather.

In 1890, Mabel Sibley Jones became the first teacher in the small, frontier town of Tajique in New Mexico Territory. She rode the train from Wilmington, Delaware and Tajique mercantile owner Elisha Dow met her in Santa Fe. He had publicized for a teacher through the Presbyterian Home Missions Society and other teacher agencies and Mabel agreed to teach in Tajique's new school.

They traveled between Santa Fe and Tajique in Elisha Dow's covered wagon. It took two days to reach Tajique and Mr. Dow stopped along the way and cooked their lunch and dinner, and they spent one night en-route. Mabel described the experience in a short story she sent to Elisha Dow in 1952. She wrote, "We stopped at a roadhouse that evening and spent the night without disrobing and slept in a room where others were resting."

The next day they drove along the eastern slopes of the Manzano Mountains reaching Tajique after midnight. "We were glad to relax in a bed. Tajique, a village east of El Bosque, built of adobe houses around a plaza, had a population of less than five hundred," she stated.

According to Mabel's short story, the town's water supply was acquired from one well and a fresh water stream running through the town. Most of the homes kept their drinking water in a vessel with a gourd for drinking. The majority of the homes had dirt floors with only a few possessing windows and doors. She wrote, "The Dow house had two residential sections with a general store occupying the center. There was ample window space in the structure." Mabel lived with the Dow family, and her room faced the plaza so she was able to observe many of the local traditions.

During this era in New Mexico's history membership in the religious society known as the Hermanos Penitentes was prevalent throughout the villages east of the Sandia and Manzano Mountains. This religious group felt they needed to give penitence for their sins by hurting themselves by wearing cactus on their backs or in their feet so they could feel the pain Jesus had felt upon the cross.

Jones wrote about the religious activities of the Penitentes, "This section of the Manzanos was a fastness especially suited to the age-old rites of the Hermanos Penitentes. The death of a prominent Penitente being announced in the village, I called upon the family. The body of the dead man was neatly attired and laying upon a table."

On a bitterly, cold night a few evenings later, Mabel walked with the women to the small cemetery nearby. "I joined the women. We marched to the tune of their songs: Penitence, Penitence, sin no more unfortunate man. The shrill notes sounded by their fife or pito were in a minor key, which caused its frequent, repetition to become monotonous and eerie. We carried lighted candles."

She described how members of the group lashed the body of a man numerous times over the grave of the deceased Penitente. She saw blood trickling from the body onto the grave. She explained how the evening ended, "The ceremony over the grave, in that isolated country, was impressive and reverential. We reached home at two o'clock in the morning."

It seems the community had a disagreement over the local election results. Mabel was concerned about what might happen next. "The rioters shot through the Dow residence through the shutters and the door of the dancehall, and tore the pilings off the front porch," she wrote. Eventually Elisha Dow had to walk outside onto the porch and shoot his pistol into the air a couple times which eventually drove away the attackers."

Wedding, funerals and fiestas were events to look forward to throughout the year for those living in Tajique. Dancing was a favorite form of entertainment for those living in the isolated mountain settlements. Dances normally started at sunset and lasted until sunrise. It was felt that it was safer to travel during the daylight hours. Mabel explains, "There was always wandering antelope, wild horses, coyotes, cattle, sheep and the redundant prairie dog."

Jones describes some of the rules and regulations upheld at these dances, "The dances were held in the larger homes or in the schoolhouse. The dances were rather conventional as the dancers not permitted to converse while dancing and were banned from the floor if they violated the dancing rules," she wrote. "If there was too much drinking by the men, the dance sometimes ended boisterously."

In the weeks leading to New Mexico's rainy season, those living in Tajique as well as along the Manzano Range would meet to pray for rain. Jones wrote, "A statue of the Virgin Mary was carried through the streets and whenever sufficient funds were available, she was carried into a home and set upon some resting place, and before this alter, prayers were offered, asking for blessings and protection for this house."

***

Mabel was able to make friends in the isolated settlement, as in 1890, the Rea family also relocated to the Tajique area and built a homestead on top of El Bosque, a high ridge in the Manzano Mountains to the west of Tajique. Archibald and Alice Rea had often gazed at the ridge from the west side of the mountain range at Isleta where Archie worked as a trader among the Isleta Indians and his wife Alice served as a nurse practitioner and herbalist. The mountaintop had appealed to them over the years.

Ambrose Douglass, Alice Rea's brother was the first to homestead atop El Bosque, but the 320-acre homestead interfered with his job as a mining engineer and he surrendered the homestead claim to the Rea family. Archie and Alice would move to the homestead with their two small children. It was a time of solitude and introspection for Alice and Archie and from the beginning they enjoyed living at the top of the Manzano Range.

Archibald Rea was not the typical homesteader, but he would spend the rest of his life living peacefully atop the ridge. He has been described as a cultured and academically-oriented English-born Irishman from Liverpool. Unfortunately, Archie had chronic rheumatism and his disease had progressed to the point where he was in great pain by the time the family moved to El Bosque limiting his physical activities. When the family moved to the ridge, Archie was carried to the top on a stretcher. The family built a small cabin of white aspen logs where they resided while proving up on the homestead. The Rea family hired seventeen Isleta Indians to build a primitive wagon road to the top of the ridge which is currently part of the Albuquerque Trail System. The family often rode horse-back into Tajique for supplies at the Dow Store or to sell their produce to local residents.

The family needed more supplies in order to run the homestead and it was decided that Alice, Archie's wife would move to Albuquerque and earn the money needed to procure what they needed and Archie would remain on the homestead and educate the children. Alice would spend a year in Albuquerque sewing elaborate gowns for the wealthy to earn the money needed for the homestead.

The Rea family possessed a well-stocked library making up one of the rooms in the small cabin. Archie educated the children in all avenues of a well-rounded education stressing the arts, math, history, literature, the sciences and even music as he was a classical violinist. His children received an education far beyond what the frontier schools in the area were teaching at the time.

When Alice returned to the homestead after her time in Albuquerque, she brought with her seeds and plows to work the soil, as well as one milk cow with calf, one horse and a mule and four burros. With these supplies the homestead was able to flourish and support the family.

A year later, Alice's three sisters and five more children moved to the mountaintop. Later, one of her sisters would marry anthropologist Charles Lummis and the other Willy Dow from Tajique. As the homestead grew, the women took care of the crops and livestock while Archie gave the seven children a top-rate education. The homestead prospered, and the Reas traded their excess crops for clothes, groceries, fruit, butter and other items needed on the homestead.

The homestead soon became a retreat for family, friends, notable writers, journalists, artists and even Teddy Roosevelt as well as famous anthropologists Adolph Bandelier and Charles Lummis. The Rea family enjoyed entertaining and their hospitality was known throughout the state and region. No matter how many unannounced guests arrived, Alice Rea always had enough food for everyone. One story states that the family often teased her about opening a restaurant so she would get paid for all her cooking.

The family was able to hire farm hands and an important convenience came to the homestead in the form of a phone line. A line was installed between El Bosque and the Dow Store in Tajique. El Bosque would also be utilized as a fire lookout station for a number of years until a more permanent structure could be built on Capilla Peak.

When Archibald passed away in 1909, Alice decided to leave her mountaintop home and move down near the canyon floor at Rancho Ojo de las Casas near the mouth of Comanche Canyon. Alice continued to care for her family until she passed away at the age of 94 in 1946. The children who had been educated by Archibald Rea always praised him for the fine education they had received on a mountaintop on the New Mexico Frontier.

***

Another pioneer teacher who taught in nearby Mountainair was Josephine Corbett Veal. She arrived in Mountainair in time to become the first assistant postmistress in 1908. By 1913, she had become the principal of the Mountainair Public School system with the additional faculty of one primary teacher. She is remembered as a tall, slim lady of aristocratic bearing. Little is known of her husband Philip Veal as their marriage was short-lived and ended in divorce.

Josephine wrote a letter describing her move to New Mexico. "Early in 1901, the AT&SF Railroad decided to open the heart of New Mexico by building a short route to the coast. My brother knew of this and due to ill health decided to come to the Southwest. He knew there would be a town here at the summit of Abo Pass. He returned here and stayed. In the spring of 1903, I decided to spend my vacation here"

She tells of her trip to Mountainair, "After so long, we reached my destination. My trunk and I landed on a platform. It was raining; a block away there was a building that might be a station. I saw no one. I stood still near my nice new wall trunk. After awhile a man with a mail pouch was coming toward. He asked if I was Miss Corbett. He said my brother had waited a long time. Then one day he had approached a trainman and asked isn't there a woman on the train from Kansas City. The answer was no, No train had left Kansas City in a week due to the big flood. He had asked the trainman to watch for me and take me to Dunlavy's home. Mr. and Mrs. Dunlavy were lovely and I stayed all night. Next morning still it rained. Mr. Dunlavy went with me to a box car, a work train on the New Mexico Central."

She was a little alarmed by the other people who came to ride in the box car. Next, she noticed a man with a long gun with a no-nonsense expression on his face. Mr. Dunlavy introduced Josephine to the sheriff and she and the sheriff rode together on the box-car. Josephine felt a lot safer with him riding next to her to her next destination.

The train arrived in Willard around noon. Her brother had sent a man to meet her there who would give her a ride into Mountainair. She wrote, "Still it rained. We waited and had refreshments. Then I bought a big red comforter; wrapped it around me; raised my umbrella; a wave to Mr. Dunlavy and we were off.

Her brother had prepared a dugout home for her and she describes its appearance upon her arrival, "My dugout home was the finest of the dugout homes. The dug-out part was five-foot-deep and 12 X 14. All around this was a shelf, a convenience for pictures, potted plants, etc. There was a cabinet above it for dishes, eats, etc. There was a cooler on the north. The walls were plastered. There were two windows and a covering over the entrance steps. The wood walls above the shelf were papered," she wrote. "There was a mock fireplace for fuel. A winding stair led to my bedroom. After I established residence, I had a beautiful Wilton velvet rug on the floor. I added a screen and it was a real parlor."

Josephine had taught in the Kansas City Schools for ten years and would spend another ten teaching in Mountainair. She was always remembered as a good teacher, who made sure her students had the skills to prepare them for life. She was instrumental in making the Mountainair Public Schools a success in the early years. She had a certain style about her that caused the children to want to excel. Josephine would spend the remainder of her life in Mountainair where she had traveled long hours on the train for her first visit and then returned to Kansas City to teach a few more years. But, the atmosphere of New Mexico pulled her back to the railroad town her brother J.W. Corbett had helped to found in 1903.

Original Mountainair High School
Author's Collection

Chapter Seven — African-American Women Who Made History

The American West was the perfect location for African-Americans wanting to make a good life for themselves and their family after the Civil War. The Emancipation Proclamation of 1863 granted many blacks freedom for the first time in their lives. Many joined together and moved to the American Frontier where there were more opportunities and less prejudice against them. Those pioneers making up frontier society were not overly concerned with race in most cases, as there were all races and nationalities living on the frontier.

Those African-Americans who were able to run away from their life of bondage often tried to make it to the American Frontier, or they joined with different Native American tribes eventually settling down and intermarrying into the tribe. They had a much better life among the Native Americans who thought of them as equal.

African-American women who moved to the American Frontier were often much different from the white women who had proceeded them. Most of the black women were in their twenties to their early forties and a lot older than the first white women arriving on the frontier. Most of the African-American women were married and were close to the end of their child bearing years.

Black women were not as interested in homesteading as the white women had been, as they associated this type of lifestyle with what they had endured back on the plantation. They preferred to work in a city settlement and there were fewer African-Americans than any other group amongst the homesteaders.

African-American women often worked as domestic servants, which was the same for white women who worked outside the home. They found they were paid much better on the frontier than they had been on the East Coast or as a freed black in the south. They were allowed to start their own businesses and they faced a lot less racial anger and violence.

Those black women who headed west also had a wider choice of husbands to choose from, as did all women on the frontier. Black men outnumbered the women as high as ten to one, and there of course was a higher percentage of marriage for those women than they had ever encountered before.

Many African-American women traveled west as mail order brides, especially in Arizona and New Mexico. The idea was suggested by married black women on the frontier as they found being outnumbered by the men to such a degree unsettling. They felt the wrong types of women were coming to town and this caused fighting amongst the men. The men living on the frontier had already gone through several wives as it was not an easy place for women especially during the initial settlement years.

***

Amelia Earhart, Charles Lindbergh, the Wright brothers and other aviation pioneers are often mentioned in the history books. Most school children know the first plane was flown at Kitty Hawk, North Carolina by the Wright brothers. But, how many know a half black and half Cherokee woman is credited with being the first woman to fly in the United States?

Bessie Coleman was born in 1892 in Atlanta, Texas, one of thirteen children born to Susan and George Coleman who worked as sharecroppers. The family was extremely poor and had little money to survive. Bessie's father deserted the family when she was nine years old. She had to work from a young age, but was able to save enough money to attend college for one year.

When she was unable to raise money for a second year in college, she decided to move to Chicago and live with her brother while looking for work. She was able to land several positions, but during this time she discovered something that would become even more important to her. She learned about daring World War I pilots and decided she would like to do the same and learn to fly.

But, she soon discovered there were no flight schools in the United States that would accept women or blacks. She found several schools in France that would accept black women. She took a French language class and soon after the end of World War I, Bessie headed to Europe to learn to fly.

She attended the Ecole d'Aviation des Freres Caudon, a flying school in Le Crotoy in northern France. She completed seven months of flight school and earned her international flight license, the first black and Native American woman to ever do so. She returned to Chicago, but soon found it was going to be harder than she had thought making a living as a pilot.

She decided her only option at the time was stunt flying, and she would need to improve her skills and learn more tricks if she wanted to make money. There was still nowhere in the United States where she could take lessons, so she returned to Europe where they were a little more open-minded. She completed another four months of training with French and German pilots.

Bessie Coleman 1922
Photo--Author's Collection

Coleman had her first performance in New York City where a large crowd enjoyed watching her stop and start her plane just before she hit the ground. She decided she had to have her own plane and traveled to Los Angeles where she bought a Curtiss JN-Four airplane more commonly known as a Jenny. The airplane company gave her a deal on the plane if she represented their company at public events.

Bessie went to Los Angeles and organized an air show. She had a little trouble with her plane when the Jenny's engine cut out shortly after it took off and crashed to the ground. She suffered a broken leg and other minor injuries during the crash, but it did not stop her from flying.

Since she had first learned to fly, Coleman had always wanted to start her own flight school. She rented an office and attempted to line up students, but she could not pay her bills and had to return to stunt flying.

She began giving lectures and showing films of her flights. She organized air shows in Florida, Georgia and other states. She was well-received and became a celebrity of sorts. She soon had enough money to purchase her own Jenny. She was encouraged by the support she felt throughout the country and still hoped to open her own flight school.

In April of 1926, Bessie was planning another air show in Jacksonville, Florida. She had recently purchased her own Jenny in Dallas. Her mechanic as well as publicity agent, William Willis, flew the plane from Dallas to Jacksonville, but had to make three forced landings along the way because the plane was worn out and had been poorly maintained.

Coleman's family and friends tried to get her to cancel the air show until she could do some serious work on the plane and make sure it was safe. Coleman laughed off their worries, and she and Willis took the plane on a flight over the air field in order to check out the field for a parachute drop Coleman planned on performing.

Willis flew the plane so Coleman could lean over to look at the field. Ten minutes into the flight, with no warning the plane took a dive then starting spinning. Coleman was thrown from the plane at 2,000 feet and died instantly upon hitting the ground. Willis was not able to gain control of the plane and it crashed to the ground and burst into flames killing him in the process. Later, it was discovered that a wrench used to service the engine had jammed the gearbox.

Bessie was only thirty-four years old when she died. Five thousand people attended a memorial for Coleman in Orlando, Florida. It was reported that 15,000 attended a second memorial when her body was returned to Chicago where she was buried.

Coleman has definitely not been forgotten though, as every April 30, African-American aviators, both men and women, fly in formation over Lincoln Cemetery in southwest Chicago where Coleman is buried and drop flowers on her grave.

A road near O'Hare International Airport was named for Coleman, as well as the U.S. Postal Service honored Coleman with a commemorative stamp. Other women followed Coleman as professional aviators and the Bessie Coleman Aviators Organization was founded by black women pilots in 1975 and is open to women pilots of all races. Her dream of a flying school for African-Americans became a reality when William J. Powell established the Bessie Coleman Aero Club in Los Angeles.

***

Another intriguing black woman was Mary Fields who was more commonly known as Stagecoach Mary. She has been described most often as standing over six feet tall and weighing two hundred pounds. She smoked homemade cigars and always carried a pair of six-shooters and a ten-gauge shotgun. She was the first African-American woman to become a stagecoach driver and carry the U.S. mail.

Mary was born a slave in the 1830s in Tennessee. When she gained her freedom, she migrated to Toledo, Ohio and found a job working for the Ursuline Convent. In 1884, the nuns founded the St. Peter's Catholic Mission School in Montana where Mary joined them three years later. She remained at the mission school for over ten years and provided protection for the nuns. She also did carpentry and whatever other work the nuns needed her to do.

Several stories have survived describing Mary's legendary temper. She actually had a shootout with one of the cowpunchers in town that left him slightly wounded and embarrassed that a woman had made him look bad. Mary did not always act in the way women were expected to act, and she was unconcerned about what people thought of her. She lost her position with the nuns because of her loud mouth and bold actions.

She would later settle in Cascade County, Montana. She opened a café and it became a popular place for local residents. Her restaurant wasn't able to meet the bills because Mary had too kind of a heart and gave away free food to those who did not have money. Most sources stated that she was not that great of a cook either. She would next survive by running a laundry, but Mary would finally find the perfect job with the U.S. Post Office. She loved the position so much that she continued working into her seventies. She possessed a certain pride on delivering the mail on schedule and was always determined to do so in all kinds of weather. When the snow was too deep, she would leave her team at home and deliver the mail on foot.

Mary was ahead of her time in many ways or maybe it was merely because she did not care what other people thought of her manner or dress. She often wore pants underneath her skirt and apron to keep warm during brutal Montana winters. She always had a gun hidden in her apron and most of the time was not bothered because those living in the community knew she could shoot and was not afraid to do so.

Artist Charles Russell once painted Mary when he lived in Cascade a short time. The drawing was titled: A Quiet Day in Cascade — the pen-and-ink sketch shows Mary being knocked down by a hog and overturning a basket of eggs.

She was loved by the community, and they often checked to make sure she was alright. They even declared her birthday a holiday and closed the school for the day. In 1914, she passed away and the whole town attended her funeral.

***

Ida B. Wells-Barnett was an educated African-American woman who lived between the years of 1862 and 1931. She was the oldest of eight children and grew up in Holly Springs, Mississippi. Her parents were actively involved in the Republican Party during Reconstruction instilling in Ida a sense of injustice for blacks in the United States.

Ida attended Rust College and then began her teaching career in Memphis, Tennessee. Ida had a problem with a white conductor on the local train when she first arrived in town. She purchased a first-class ticket and was sitting in that section when the conductor asked her to move. She refused, and when the conductor tried to move her forcefully she fought back. She was eventually ejected from the train.

She sued the train where she won her case in the lower courts but lost in the upper court system. This experience would cause her to look into a career in Journalism. She became a co-owner and editor of a black newspaper called *The Free Speech and Headlight*. She wrote passionate articles about violence against blacks, poor schools and about black people not standing up for themselves. She especially wrote articles against senseless lynching imposed upon black people during this era in American history.

In 1892, three of Ida's friends were lynched. They were Henry Stewart, Thomas Moss and Calvin McDowell who were co-owners of the People's Grocery Company. White businesses in the area claimed the small store had taken away much of their business. A group of white men decided they would eliminate the competition. They attacked the store, but the owners fought back and killed one of the attackers. Stewart, Moss and McDowell were arrested and put in jail, but later that evening an angry mob broke into the jail, took them outside and lynched them before they had a chance for a fair trial.

The lynching of African-Americans during this era in United States History is shameful and embarrassing a hundred years later. But, Ida was not afraid to stand up for what was happening to her people, even when the newspaper office where she worked was destroyed by a group of white men. Her life was threatened unless she quit writing articles about the lynching of her three friends.

She decided to move to Chicago where she helped develop and organize several African American women and reform organizations. But, she could never forget the lynching of her three innocent friends and it remained the focus of her writing. She continued to write articles on the injustice of lynching black men, which had become a common practice throughout the South. She also became involved in the women's suffrage movement, as women of all races were discriminated against during these years in the southern states too.

Ida was outspoken and not afraid to stand up for black rights and ahead of her time for a black woman in the United States. She crusaded against illegal lynching of black men and the injustice of segregation of the races. It was a terrifying time for African-Americans and there was little they could do about the injustice during this time in history. They had to be on constant guard and make sure they were not in the wrong place when a crime occurred. It was easy during these years to put the blame on a black man and walk away.

***

Lucretia Marchbanks was born a slave on a Tennessee plantation in 1832. Lucretia's father was a half brother to the plantation owner Martin Marchbanks and enjoyed special privileges because of the relationship. Lucretia was the eldest of eleven children and belonged to a respected African-American family. She was trained in the culinary arts and housekeeping and worked in the plantation house the years she was a slave.

More recently, Lucretia was portrayed as Aunt Lou in the mini-series on Deadwood, South Dakota. Her story and character in the series describes her as the most popular cook during Deadwood's rip-roaring mining years. Not only was she a good cook, but she had a way with money and started saving for the ranch she had always wanted.

When younger Lucretia had traveled to California with her master's daughter and while there she observed the gold rush spirit and way in which the miners freely spent their money. She decided she would live in one of these types of communities and try her hand at making money and established a successful business in Deadwood.

She traveled to Dakota Territory where she joined in the gold rush already going strong. She arrived in the mining town in June of 1876 where she easily gained employment at the Frontier Hotel as a cook and housekeeper. Everyone who met "Aunt Lou" could see the hard working and honest woman she was and she soon made friends and no one felt any prejudice toward her as she had felt back in Tennessee.

Later, she would work as the manager of the hotel at the DeSmet Mine where she worked for four different superintendents for $40.00 a month, a small salary for all the work she did and when compared to what the miners had to pay to spend the night. She went on to work for Harry Gregg where she remained until 1883 when she opened her own establishment the Rustic Hotel. She has often been referred to as the finest cook in the Black Hills. One of her favorite dishes to prepare was plum puddings. She would never give anyone the recipe when they asked for it.

Aunt Lou had also learned important nursing and mid-wife skills needed in a frontier community such as Deadwood. She nursed many in the mining town during the mountain fever epidemic and won the respect of everyone in the community.

In 1880 the mining town threw a festival in order to raise money to build a Congregational Church and a prize of a large, diamond ring would be auctioned off and given to the most popular women in Deadwood. Aunt Lou won the diamond ring easily with few competitors getting near her number of votes.

Aunt Lou decided to retire from the successful business she had established as the Rustic Hotel and purchased a ranch at Rockyford, just across the border near present-day Beulah. She had always wanted to raise horses and cattle. A ranch-hand named George Baggely worked for her for over twenty years and they are presently buried next to one another in the Beulah Cemetery. Aunt Lou passed away in 1911.

Chapter Eight — Frontier Women
Taken Captive

Note from Author: While a middle school student back in the 1960s, I discovered the book *Indian Captive* by Lois Lenski. The book is about Mary Jamison who was captured by the Shawnee Indians when she was twelve years old in 1758. This book made a great impression on my young mind, as it caused me to seriously consider what it would be like to be taken into captivity by a Native American tribe while traveling throughout the American Frontier.

The book was heart-breaking in the beginning, especially the scene where Jamison is separated from her family and forced to accompany the Shawnee without them. Her family would be massacred shortly after her departure but fortunately for her she was not aware of what happened to them at the time. Even though, the incident occurred over two hundred years ago, I still feel bad for Mary Jamison and what she had to endure during her childhood.

The Jamison family settled on a tract of land known as Marsh Creek in Adams County, Pennsylvania. They were a hard working and prosperous family and established a nice farm where they lived for eight years. Mary's two oldest brothers were able to escape, but the remainder of Mary's family was taken captive and spent one night on the trail before the remainder of the family was massacred except for Mary.

The Shawnee would soon trade Mary to two sisters from the Seneca Tribe who had lost a brother and Mary would become a member of their family for the rest of her life. She did not leave even when she had the opportunity to escape. The tribe lived in the western part of what is now New York. Mary was often called the White Woman of the Genesse, she had two Seneca husbands, children, her own home and garden. She was happy living with the Seneca.

***

For those women traveling on the American Frontier in the 19th Century, it was more than possible that they could be abducted by one of the Native American tribes roaming the area. Some women and children were captured while the men were away hunting or working in the fields, while in other cases the men were killed first while the women and children hid and watched the massacre.

Native American tribes took captives for various reasons. They wanted to replace members of their family or tribe who had been killed. Sometimes the captives were used as slaves and traded to other tribes or used as a bargaining chip against those invading their land. Many times captives died while in captivity while others became part of the tribe, married and had children often forgetting their native language and customs. There were many captives that did not want to return to their families while others tried to escape and return to civilization as soon as possible.

Olive Oatman
Photo--Author's Collection

The tragedy of the Oatman family occurred along the banks of the Gila River seventy miles from Fort Yuma, Arizona in 1851 and was one of the most publicized accounts of a Native American raid and abduction. After watching the massacre of six members of their family, Olive at age fourteen and Mary Ann at age eight were taken into captivity by the Yavapai. Lorenzo, age fifteen was left for dead.

Lorenzo heard the screams of Olive and Mary Ann as the Yavapai forced them onto the back of their horses before passing out. When he gained consciousness later, he found the rest of his family had been massacred. The girls saw their brother shot down and thought he was dead and they were the only two remaining alive.

Olive's parents were not pioneer material and should have remained in a more civilized section of the country. They did not possess wilderness skills and were unable to protect themselves along the trail. They had problems from the beginning and had placed their trust in a self-proclaimed seer named James Colin Brewster who had branched off from the teachings of Brigham Young. He had organized a wagon train consisting of a group of people who wanted to start their own community at the confluence of the Gila and Colorado Rivers and form a settlement called land of Bashan. Those Mormons joining the wagon train and following Brewster's teachings were called Brewsters.

Many of the others traveling in the wagon train did not care for Olive's father. He did not always follow the rules of the wagon train and argued with the other Mormons. His family soon started to travel outside the wagon train, which was not a good idea as groups traveling alone were sometimes massacred.

The family would spend a miserable final night together when they got stuck in quick sand and pulled their wagons out onto a sand bar in the Gila River. The next day a group of starving Yavapai happened upon them. They asked the Oatman's for food and water which they had very little of and were trying to ration to keep from running out. But, they gave the Yavapai what they had. But, when the Native Americans asked for more they said they had to save what they had for the family. The Yavapai started screaming and yelling while they clubbed the family to death and pillaged through their food supplies.

After the massacre, the Yavapais took what supplies were left and forced Olive and Mary Ann to accompany them. The first year of their captivity was the hardest for the girls as the Yavapai used the sisters as slaves and treated them with disdain and brutality. But, at the end of their first year of captivity Olive and Mary Ann were traded to the Mojave tribe for a few vegetables, blankets and horses.

The girls moved with the Mohave Indians to a location near present-day Needles, California. They were lucky to be adopted into the family of one of the tribal leaders where they experienced more humane treatment. Before long they felt like they were part of the family.

Olive and Mary Ann believed they would never make it back to any type of civilization like they had known before. They felt there was nothing left to return to since their entire family had been massacred. They had no idea their brother Lorenzo had survived and was trying to find and rescue them. Before long they became assimilated into the tribe and soon forgot much of their native language and family traditions.

They spoke Mohave and dressed in their style of clothing and adopted the habits and customs of the tribe. The Mohave culture believed in tattoos, so they would be recognized by their relatives in their after-life and they often tattooed their chins, arms and legs. Both Olive and Mary Ann had their chins tattooed as this was a sign that they had been accepted as members of the tribe.

The American Southwest experienced numerous periods of drought during the years the Oatman sisters lived with the Mojave. In 1855, many members of the tribe passed away of starvation as did Olive's sister Mary Ann. It was hard for Olive to lose her sister especially since she believed she was the last member of her family. She buried her sister and was often seen mourning over her grave. Mary Ann had never been able to handle the life that was imposed upon her.

But, Lorenzo had not given up in his quest to find his sisters. He traveled to California and continued searching and seeking information and support with the search. Finally, a messenger was sent out from Fort Yuma to the Mohave tribe. A Yuma Indian was sent to talk to the Mohave about their captive, and he told the tribe those in authority knew Olive was living with them and they were to send her to Fort Yuma to avoid problems.

In 1855, after spending five years living with the Native Americans, Olive was taken from the Mojave and sent to Fort Yuma where she was reunited with her brother Lorenzo. When she first arrived at the fort, she refused to speak since she had forgotten most of her native language. She was wearing a bark skirt and other Mojave clothing upon her arrival, but the women at the fort felt she should change into something more suitable.

Lorenzo and Olive moved to southern Oregon for a few years where they met R.B. Stratton, a Methodist minister who convinced the Oatmans to allow him to write a book about their experiences. The *Captivity of the Oatman Girls* was an immediate success upon its first publication in San Francisco in 1857 and quickly became a best-seller. The book was one of the few published narratives anyone had ever written on spending time in captivity with a Native American tribe.

The Oatman siblings went on the lecture circuit and sold Stratton's book while telling of their experiences. They made enough money to pay for their educations at the University of the Pacific in Oregon. Upon their graduation, they moved to New York with Stratton and Olive gave lectures throughout the city. She normally wore a veil over her face so the tattoos would not be visible, but while she lectured she took off the veil and allowed the public to see her face.

While lecturing in Michigan, Olive met John Fairchild, a wealthy ranch owner and farmer from Rochester, New York. They were married in 1865. Olive quit the lecture circuit and burned all the books she had about her life in captivity. Several sources point out that it was actually her husband John who burned the books. Whatever the true story, she would never lecture about her captivity again.

The couple adopted a baby girl and named her Mamie, and they lived in a nice, two-story house. They moved to Sherman, Texas and Olive became a respected member of the community. Yet, she spent most of her time at home alone and rarely interacted with other people. Her five years in captivity had changed her, as it would change any woman.

Some historians think Olive was happy with the Mohave and had married a member of the tribe and they had several children although this has never been proven. She never talked much about this family in her lectures. But, maybe she was quiet because she was thinking about the two different families she had lost in her life. She always spoke highly of the Mohave and seemed to mourn for them the rest of her life. Olive passed away in Sherman, Texas in 1903.

***

In 1981, John Wright, the son of Ed and Maud Wright wrote an article for the *Torrance County Citizen* about his mother Maud's nine days as the captive of Pancho Villa during the ill-fated Columbus Raid in 1916. Johnny, who was only a child at the time, was left at his parents' ranch with the Mexican couple who worked for the Wrights.

Although, Maud would spend most of her life in New Mexico, she was born in Alabama in 1889 to Tom and Belle Hawk. Since she was the only daughter out of five children, she learned to work like a man in her growing up years. Maud was also known for her handling of horses and mules, as she was often better at handling them than the men.

By year 1900, the Hawk family had moved to Oklahoma where they made a living by logging. Maud worked alongside her brothers in the family business. A young sawyer by the name of Ed Wright noticed Maud and was soon trying to strike up a conversation with her, but her father was not interested in his best worker leaving him with no hands to work his logging operations, so he discouraged the relationship between the two. He had been thinking about moving to New Mexico and decided this might be a good time to slow down the relationship between the two young people.

But, Ed was not one to give up. He started to look for opportunities to support a family and found it south of the border in Mexico. Wright explained his father's plans, "Many Americans were going to Mexico where they believed a good opportunity awaited them," he wrote. "Ed was both energetic and conservative. He prospered and soon purchased a small ranch and set up a saw-mill thirty miles from Pearson in the state of Chihuahua. With this accomplished he returned to the states in search of Maud."

Maud's family was living in Pinos Altos near Silver City when Ed caught up with them. He went back to sawyer work and renewed his pursuit of Maud. Maud's father would still not consent to the marriage although Maud was of an age to marry if she wanted to do so. Wright explains, "They decided to elope. They rode first by horseback and then by stage to El Paso where they were married in January of 1910," he pointed out. "From there they went by train to Pearson where Ed bought a wagon and team as well as household goods and supplies."

Ed and Maud were happy on their ranch in Mexico, and Maud soon took over much of the ranch work with the assistance of their hired hand Augustino Marino. Marino and his wife lived nearby. Ed was able to get his sawmill up and running with the help of Frank Hayden and several Mexican laborers.

During this era in Mexico's history, Pancho Villa and his revolutionists were causing havoc throughout Mexico. The family had lived peacefully on their ranch for over a year before they had their first encounter with this violent group. They stopped by the ranch after one of their raids and left their exhausted horses and took Wright's fresh ones without asking or paying for them. The raids became so bad for a time that the Wrights and many of their neighbors returned to the United States in 1913 until the violence and unrest in Mexico could be brought under control.

On March 1, 1916, Maud was cooking dinner for Ed and Frank Hayden, as she was expecting them to return soon from a trip to Pearson where they had gone for supplies. She heard the sound of horses and went out to meet them. She soon discovered over fifty Mexican soldiers under the command of Pancho Villa had invaded her yard. When the group demanded food, she gave them what she had been preparing.

When Ed and Frank returned to the ranch leading two pack mules, they were immediately surrounded by the Mexicans and their supplies confiscated. The Mexicans asked Ed and Frank if they had anything they could feed the horses and they went to the barn. When they failed to return to the house Maud became worried.

Others returned to the house and demanded to see what supplies the Wrights had, and then they went through the house taking what supplies they needed and trashed the house in the process. She was told to leave her son Johnnie behind with Mrs. Marino and told her to get on the horse behind him, but she refused to do what he asked and walked to the top of the hill nearby to look for Ed and Frank.

Johnnie explained what happened next, "There was a saddle horse without a rider, and the Mexican leader demanded that she get on this horse and come with them," he wrote. "That was when she realized that she was being taken captive. They would not let her return to the house but gave orders to start marching right then."

Near daylight on March 2, after riding horse-back all night, the group arrived at Cave Valley where Villa was camped with his main army. The army was camped up and down the canyon for a mile or so. Maud noticed they had stolen all of the Wright's horses and mules as she identified them among the vast herd.

During the endless night, Maud was worried about the fate of Ed and Frank, and it was not until they arrived at Villa's camp that she was able to see them for the last time. Johnnie writes about the encounter, "A detail of three men came by leading a horse on which both Ed and Frank were riding, both with their hands tied behind them. This was the first time she had really known that Ed and Frank were still alive, and was also the first indication that Ed had that she was a prisoner."

They only had a brief few minutes to speak to one another as the men passed, but they discussed if either one of them could get away, they should go back for Johnnie and then get across the border and remain in the United States. She saw them go behind a nearby hill and later the Mexicans returned without the two men and she never saw them again.

Maud, who was fluent in Spanish, heard the men discussing a raid into the United States at the Columbus border crossing. She was forced once again to get on a horse and ride with the raiding party toward the United States. They soon encountered another raiding party driving thirty head of cattle and stopped to camp for the night. They butchered the cattle and cooked the meat over the campfires during the evening. Maud was offered a piece of dirty meat burned on the outside and raw in the middle, but she was unable to eat the first night of her captivity. The left-over meat was tied behind their saddles to eat later.

She was given a piece of partially cooked meat to tie behind her saddle, and before the nine days of her captivity had passed, she ate the meat as that was the only food she was offered. They did not cover the meat and it was full of dirt and horse hair. When they ran out of beef they butchered their mules and horses.

The group rode hard each day and only stopped at night to rest or to butcher and cook more beef. When they stopped for an afternoon rest, Villa would call his men together and they would sit in the shade and discuss their raiding plans. Maud overheard Villa telling his men that when they took possession of the United States they could all be rich.

The first two to three days Maud was with the group she was suffering from shock and did not pay attention like she would when they got closer to the United States border. Maud had a brief opportunity to ask Villa about his plans for her, and he said if she could make it to Columbus then he would set her free. Maud knew from the way he was speaking that he truly did not think she was tough enough to make it that long.

Maud had only one chance to escape during her nine day ordeal. Johnny explains what happened, "Down in an arroyo she saw a saddled horse grazing. She tried desperately to catch him, thinking maybe she could escape on him," he wrote. "The pony was half bronkish and would not let her get close enough to touch him." She was noticed by the Mexicans and stopped before she could ride off. Villa told her he would kill her the next time she tried to escape and this made her think about Johnny back at the ranch, and she decided she would do what they asked.

Maud was left with the horse herd when the group rode off for Columbus. When Villa's group was defeated and pushed back into Mexico, Villa let Maud go and told her to ride to Columbus and give herself over to the Americans. Before arriving in Columbus she rode upon a ranch and stopped to water the horse and herself. When she dismounted she noticed a dead man on the ground and heard moans coming from behind the ranch house, and when she investigated she discovered a Mrs. Moore who had been shot through the hip. She helped her back to the house and tried to make her comfortable. American soldiers showed up and took Maud into custody.

At first it was thought she might be a spy for Pancho Villa and she was questioned until they were sure she was innocent. She was taken to the home of Colonel Slocum and his wife who was in charge of the Army post at Columbus.

Johnnie explains what happened next, "Mrs. Slocum was very kind and sympathetic, providing her own fresh clothes and helping her to get cleaned up. Her hands face, and feet especially her feet were so swollen and sore that it was painful for them to be touched."

Maud & Johnny in 1916
Photo--John Wright Photo

Mexican President Carranza apologized for the Columbus Raid, as well as made arrangements for a special train to go to Pearson and bring Johnny to El Paso to this mother. The authorities found the bodies of Ed and Frank where Maud had told them they would be located. On March 10, 1916 Mrs. Slocum accompanied Maud on the train to El Paso to be reunited with her son.

Johnnie wrote in the article, "Mrs. Augustine Moreon had taken Johnny to Pearson, arriving there on the same day of the Columbus Raid. When the officers located her and wanted to take Johnny, she refused to surrender him without authority from Maud, and told them that Mrs. Wright had asked her to take care of Johnny until she returned."

Colonel and Mrs. Slocum gave Maud money for a train ticket to Silver City, New Mexico where her brother lived. A few weeks later, she and Johnnie moved to Stafford, Arizona and lived with her parents. While in Stafford, she met Will Medders and they married in August of 1917 and they moved to Mountainair where they became pinto bean farmers and ranchers. Maud would have seven more children with Will, two sons and five daughters.

Maud went on with the rest of her life, but she never forgot the nine days she was the captive of Pancho Villa and lost her husband and ranch in Mexico.

Chapter Nine –Women Fire Lookouts

Note from author: I have spent over thirty seasons "looking out" for forest fires throughout the American West. Upon accepting my first lookout job on Bearwallow Fire Lookout on New Mexico's Gila National Forest, I very quickly became addicted to the peaceful and self-sufficient lifestyle. For someone who has always felt they were born a century too late, the job, from the beginning was the perfect one for me. Fire Lookouts live a primitive lifestyle for three to six months each year similar in many ways to what the American pioneers would have experienced. Those people working as fire lookouts expect to spend months alone in the wilderness looking for wildfire with only the birds and wildlife for company. Many do not last one season while others return to their wilderness post year after year and would never consider working anywhere else.

In the 1990s, I staffed fire lookouts on the Black Hills National Forest on both the South Dakota and Wyoming sides of the forest. I love the Great Plains, the rugged mountains on the Wyoming side and the history of the Black Hills region. Most of the fire seasons were extremely active, and I have never seen lightning as intense as that in the Black Hills. I remember sitting on the floor with my head in my hands during my first lightning storm on Warren Peak but I soon became acclimated to the lightning storms and looked forward to their arrival. I will forever miss the Bearlodge Mountains in northeast Wyoming where I served as a fire lookout for a decade.

In 2002, I returned to New Mexico and the Manzano Mountains of my childhood where I have staffed Capilla Peak Fire Lookout for the past twelve years. The Manzano Range has experienced devastating fires in the past few years, but the land is beginning to return to its former beauty. The Manzano Mountains always remained in my heart when I worked in other areas of the country, and I planned on returning home one day and working Capilla Peak in my home mountains.

New Mexico's Cibola National Forest has the best lookout co-workers I have ever worked with, and they are like family. They are an extremely dedicated group of individuals who have staffed their mountaintops for decades and are accurate and helpful when reporting wildfire. They also watch out for one another in case of an emergency.

Most people do not realize the long hours and days a fire lookout spends glassing for wildfire. It is not uncommon to work twelve to fifteen hour days, six to seven days a week. There are times when fires are popping on all four districts making up the Cibola NF at the same time, and there are other days and even weeks that go by and there is little fire traffic on the Forest Service radio.

During the "Dog Days of Summer" the days appear endless with nothing to see but dust devils spinning against the cloudless sky. The days are non-ending and I feel chained to my lookout chair and binoculars. The days tend to run into one another prompting me to look at a calendar to remember what day of the week it is. I am constantly scanning and rescanning the forest and plains beyond for wildfire, a task that consumes my days and weeks. There's nothing but land, sky, the fire lookout and U.S. Forest Service radio.

But knowing my lookout colleagues are all doing the same as me and experiencing their own endless days scanning the forest, makes me not feel lonely. They too are searching for that tiny wisp of smoke that signals the start of a new fire. The lookout personnel on the Cibola NF have worked together for decades and are a "well-oiled" team. The forest continues to staff nine fire lookouts each fire season.

The Cibola NF has produced an exceptional team of fire lookouts who are known state-wide for their lookout skills. The story of two retired Cibola lookouts will be discussed later in the chapter: Karen Howell who staffed Withington Fire Lookout and Cindy Bourgeois, both of which were dedicated and accurate fire observers who have been missed since their retirements.

I cannot write a book about adventuresome women without including a section about the women who spent months alone in the wilderness reporting wildfire. They too were pioneers and had to make their way in a man's world. The United States was just coming out of the Victorian Era, and working as a fire lookout was not considered an appropriate job for women. Most U.S. Forest Service districts refused to hire women during the early years.

Fortunately, as the decades unfolded more and more women were hired as the primary lookout on fire towers. Throughout the nation, generally the lookout positions seem to be filled by half women and half men. On the Cibola NF there are currently six men and two women but that has not always been the case.

Women are often considered better suited to the life of a fire lookout than men, because they are content to read or work on their hobbies and can occupy their time. Times have changed since the first lookouts were expected to find and extinguish the fires they spotted and women fire lookouts have shown they are perfectly capable of performing lookout duties. Modern day towers often possess electricity and conveniences not available to earlier fire lookouts. Women will continue to play an important role in the history of fire lookouts. They have always been an integral and respected part of the fire detection system.

I want to dedicate this chapter of the book to my lookout colleagues and friends on the Cibola NF. They are Linda on Gallinas Lookout west of Corona, Joe on Withington in the San Mateo Mountains, Harold on Davenport in the Datil Range, Steve on Oso Ridge in the Zuni Mountains, Andrew on McGaffey near Bluewater Lake south of Gallup and Brian the relief fire lookout on the Mt. Taylor District plus two past lookouts Karen Howell and Cindy Bourgeois. I have spent many wonderful years working with you and think you're the most professional and dedicated fire lookouts I have ever worked with during my long career as a fire lookout. The job would not be half as fun without you!

Hallie M. Daggett — First Woman Fire Lookout
U.S. Forest Service Photo

In the early years of the U.S. Forest Service, women were not considered qualified to work as fire lookouts for the agency. It was feared they would not be able to tolerate the isolation nor be capable of the work required of the position. They would surely be afraid of the wild animals that roamed the forest, as well as storms and lightning that would pound the lookout.

Until 1913, women had only served as relief lookouts for their husbands who were hired to staff the lookout site. In those days, some positions required the lookout to extinguish the fires they spotted. The lookout's wife would staff the lookout in his absence while he searched for the fire. Women were not hired for a primary lookout position until California's Klamath National Forest hired Hallie Daggett to staff Eddy's Gulch Fire Lookout atop Klamath Peak in May of 1913.

Hallie was the perfect woman to pave the way for other women to be able to work as a fire lookout. She loved the outdoors, was familiar with the territory, she enjoyed the isolation of her lookout home and was an exceptionally dedicated and competent fire lookout. She turned in forty fires her first season and pinpointed them all when they were still small, enabling the crews to stop the fires before they got out of control. She was praised for her dedication and accuracy in reporting forest fires.

Hallie and her sister Leslie were well-educated for women of their era, as both had attended girls' seminaries in Alameda and San Francisco, California. But, upon finishing their educations they had a desire to return to their childhood home near the Black Bear Mine, run by their father and the town of Sawyer's Bar located in the Salmon River Drainage of northern California.

They were familiar with the rugged Siskiyou Mountains where they had been raised and often explored the trails with their brother Ben. All three children had learned to ride horseback plus shoot, hunt and fish while young. Hallie was a good marksman and an avid trapper and had little fear of the wild animals she encountered.

Hallie accepted the first job offered to a woman as a fire lookout and then remained at her post for fifteen years. She has often been described as the best fire lookout the U.S. Forest Service ever hired on Klamath Peak. When the public discovered a woman was working as a fire lookout for the first time, there were many newspapers and motion-picture companies that approached Hallie for details of her story. She presented lectures during her time off about her job as a fire lookout and they were heavily attended by other women seeking the same sort of adventure.

In 1983, an interesting article was written in *Women in Forestry* by Rosemary Holsinger discussing Hallie's life. Holsinger gives a description of Hallie in the article, "She was tall, strong and sunburned, with a breezy air that identified her as an outdoor dweller," she wrote.

Hallie and her siblings had been born of pioneer stock, as her father was a noted miner and politician who had crossed the Isthumus of Panama in 1852 in search of gold in California. Later, he settled in the San Francisco area in 1854. Hallie's mother Alice was born in Hannibal, Missouri and came west in a wagon train led by her father William Green.

Hallie's father became part owner and superintendent of the Black Bear Mine. The mine received its name from the abundance of black bear in the area and near the town of Sawyer's Bar. Mr. Daggett would later be elected to the state assembly and then as Lieutenant Governor of California.

Hallie had a hard time understanding why most people felt she would be afraid of living alone on a mountaintop. She had the telephone and her pets for company. She enjoyed watching the varied weather conditions sweep in from the Pacific Ocean, as well as observing animals near her lookout station. She had seven pet chipmunks that would eat out of her hand one she had raised on condensed milk that would raid her pockets for something to eat. In pictures taken of her during her time as a fire lookout, she is often pictured with a dog that lived with her on their mountain perch during the summer months.

There were also visitors who stopped by the lookout, and her sister came up once a week to bring water, supplies and mail. It was normally a three hour hike into Eddy's Gulch. Also, curious prospectors, hunters and hikers would stop in to see the first woman lookout and how she managed to survive alone on the peak.

Hallie knew she had to prove herself worthy as a fire lookout, as her hiring had often been touted as a mere experiment. She did not want to let down the district officers who had given her the chance nor ruin the opportunities for other women who would follow her in the profession. Her main duties were to scan the forest for wildfire and report her findings by telephone to the main office at Sawyer's Bar.

Hallie cut her own wood for the stove in the lookout cabin where she resided when not on lookout duty. There was plenty of wood in those days around the lookout and she did not mind getting a little exercise and cutting her own firewood. There was no need to pack in water as there was a fresh stream nearby, and in the beginning of the season she gathered snow with a shovel and bucket and melted it for her water needs. She was paid $840.00 for the entire fire season and received two days off a month if she was lucky. She often played solitaire during the day, but made sure she often glassed for fires.

Hallie dressed as a wilderness ranger when traveling back and forth to the fire lookout. She wore a heavy shirt and knickers, but while living atop the mountain she often wore ankle-length skirts and shirt-waists. She even wore a revolver strapped to her belt after seeing a panther one evening near the lookout, so she was prepared for future emergencies she might encounter.

Hallie retired from her post in 1927. In the 1950s, residents from Hallie's hometown in Etna, California built her a cabin on Main Street next to the home of her sister. She would live in the cabin until her death in 1964. Later, the cabin was donated to the city of Etna in 1993 for a park and historic site. The history of Hallie's years as a fire lookout will not soon be forgotten.

***

Another early fire lookout often referred to as the first lady lookout is Colorado's Helen Dowe. She began her first lookout season with the Pike National Forest in 1919 six years after Hallie Daggett had made the news as the first woman fire lookout. Helen also became an excellent fire lookout and did an outstanding job proving women were as good as the men who had served in the position before them. Helen had also worked as a newspaper reporter in Denver before accepting the position as a fire lookout.

Helen Dowe – Second woman to serve as a fire Lookout-- U.S. Forest Service photo

The *Routt County Republican* newspaper mentioned the lookout efforts by Helen Dowe in December of 1920, "Following two successful seasons, during which pretty Miss Helen Dowe of this city (Denver), in her capacity of forest fire lookout, has discovered more than a score of incipient blazes, officials of the National Forest service are convinced that women are equally qualified as men in the art of chasing down tiny wisps of smoke that sometimes lead to serious conflagrations in the thickly wooded districts of the Rocky Mountains."

In May of 1921, Miss Dowe is mentioned once again in another local newspaper describing how she had gone out with a U.S. Forest Service survey crew and was the first woman in the history of the United States to do so. She often worked as a scenic artist for the Denver division of the Forest Service during the winter months when not in the fire tower.

Helen Dowe on Devil's Head Fire Lookout
U.S. Forest Service Photo

***

Although, the history of New York State does not normally belong to the pages of history books about America's final frontier, the stories about the women who staffed their fire lookout towers does. They were truly adventuresome women in every sense of the word; as well as, outdoorsy, self-sufficient, intelligent women.

All the fire towers in New York's Adirondack Mountains are closed now and many have been removed from the mountain peaks where they once served in the prevention of wildfire, but when Frances Boone staffed Mt. Electra in 1942, they still graced the mountaintops. At one time, there were fifty-one fire lookouts staffed throughout the Adirondack Range.

Frances was hired as a waitress in the summer of 1940 at Forest Lodge on Lake Lila, where the Webb family had a private preserve. She became acquainted with the Webb family and the fire wardens who patrolled the area for fire, and she would later be offered the fire observer position on Mt. Electra.

Frances was excited about her new position as a fire lookout and on a spring morning she rode the train to Nehasane, the Webb family private preserve dressed in a red-plaid shirt and wearing hiking boots. She brought along her bow and arrows for practicing archery and a bicycle to ride to the trail head near the small cabin where she would live for the summer.

Post Card of Fire Lookout on Bald Mountain
Central Adirondack Mountains

The duties of fire lookouts at that time differ from the ones adhered to presently. Frances wrote about the duties in the book *Nehasane Fire Observer an Adirondack Woman's Summer of '42*, "You'll need to make out weekly reports for the Conservation Department in Albany. . .You will be expected to put in an eight-hour day at the tower, seven days a week if the weather is dry. If it rains and there is no lightning you may have one or more days off."

She was instructed to test her telephones every day at both the cabin and fire tower, as this was before the use of radios for communications became more prevalent a decade later. She rode her bike to the trailhead each morning and hiked on to the lookout tower from there. Included in her responsibilities was to keep the grass cut along the trail, with a scythe. Frances' supervisor had showed her how to use this too, as well as how to keep it sharp.

When Frances first saw the 75 foot tower she had agreed to staff for the summer, she was a little intimidated by the height but refused to let her supervisor know it. She wrote, "As I stood looking up at it, I wondered if I would trip and fall or lose my balance on those open stairs," she stated. "The skimpy railings did not seem to offer much protection either. A drink of water from the flask refreshed me and I saw Mr. Collier give me a challenging look. I made up my mind that I wasn't going to be intimidated."

She soon became acclimated to her home and new position. There was only running cold water at her cabin, so she had to start a fire in her woodstove and heat water each day for her cleaning and cooking needs. The cabin had no electricity and she preserved her perishable food in a crook submerged in the stream nearby. During her first month at the cabin, she did not even have a (musical) radio for company but made a phone call two or three times a week to catch up on the news. Later, her father would give her a radio that provided company and enjoyment for the remainder of the season.

She wrote about her days at the lookout, 'I found I was seldom bored. Whether it was scanning the magnificent forests all around, sketching a favorite view or reading a magazine, I kept track of all my activities in a little journal," she wrote. "If I wanted some exercise I descended the tower and practiced my archery."

Frances would attend art school, marry afterwards and never return to staff Mt. Electra yet she always cherished the memory. She wrote about her last day to work as a fire lookout, "I would long remember one last perfect day on the mountain. The glory of the fall season was all around me," she stated. "Without a cloud in the sky, radiant sunshine spread over the country side with a warm glow. Not a breeze ruffled the mirror-like surfaces of any pond or lake I could see."

Frances would later find employment as a fashion artist for the *Albany Times* newspaper where she drew detailed illustrations that were used as advertisements for the newspaper. While in Albany she joined the Adirondack Mountain Club and went on weekend camping trips in the mountain range where she had served as a fire lookout.

She married Howard Seaman in 1946 and by 1947 wrote numerous historical articles about the town and surrounding area. She was honored with the Founder's Award recognizing her work on the preservation of the history of the region. She was also instrumental in documenting and locating the steamer Buttercup at the bottom of Long Lake where it sunk in 1885.

Mt. Electra Fire Lookout was a privately owned and operated fire tower located on the private preserve of the Webb family. The lookout was originally named Rock Lake Fire Lookout, but was renamed Electra after Mr. Webb's wife. The lookout is no longer in use and was torn down in the 1990s by the state of New York.

Two other women had served as lookouts on Mt. Electra before Frances. Harriet Rega served as the lookout between 1924 and 1929 and Emily Ellerby served two seasons in 1930 and 1931. The private landowner, as well as the state of New York paid the wages for the fire lookout. The owner of the private preserve selected the fire observer.

***

Karen Howell and Cindy Bourgeois were legendary fire lookouts who spent decades on their mountaintops reporting forest fires on the Cibola National Forest. Karen staffed Withington in the San Mateo Mountains for twenty-two years and Cindy Bourgeois staffed Cedro in the Sandia Range for twenty-three years.

Karen began her fire lookout career in 1983 when she was hired as a relief lookout by the U.S. Forest Service headquartered in Magdalena. She staffed Davenport Lookout between Datil and Pie Town for five years, and spent another year as the lookout at Grassy Lookout on the south end of the district before making a name for herself on the Cibola National Forest's highest lookout Mt. Withington. Karen and Cindy both developed a reputation for accuracy in spotting and reporting wildfire, in some cases down to the quarter section of the quarter section a hundred miles in the distance.

Cindy's began her lookout career on Gallinas Lookout west of Corona, then went on to fill in as the relief lookout on the Mountainair District where she staffed both Gallinas and Capilla before moving on to Cedro Peak where she would spend the rest of her lookout career.

Karen pointed out, "I felt untrained and unprepared for my first lookout experience but was helped through the season by Vida Trujillo the lookout on Withington and my mentor and friend," she stated.

Karen and her husband Dan, who also worked as a fire lookout, have lived in Hawaii since Karen retired from lookout duty. "I plan on returning to lookout duty someday," she added about her life as a fire lookout.

Spending weeks sometimes months alone on an isolated lookout tower is not for everyone, but it suited Howell for almost three decades, "I read a book about fire lookouts, and it sounded like a job I would enjoy. Then I just happened to be at the right place at the right time when I found my first lookout job," Karen stated.

Karen as most fire lookouts that make the job a career, love working as a fire lookout and would not consider doing anything else, although the job is a seasonal position lasting between 3-6 months. "The job has given me meaning and purpose plus I enjoy the peaceful beauty of the forest," Karen replied when asked about the reasons for working as a fire lookout.

"The past few years I've had a bear hang out most mornings and evenings. One day while I was looking for berries during my lunch walk I came so close to the bear that we almost touched noses. We were both so surprised that we ran in opposite directions. I hope the bear will be alright," commented Karen.

Karen commented upon making the decision to give up her long-time mountain home, "I will miss everything about this lookout station. It has been home for over twenty years. I'll think about the summers I turned in six to eight fires a day. The Coffee Pot Complex is something I will never forget. The growth of the fire during a hot, dry June and all the hard work of the firefighters plus all that smoke covering the land. I will often remember the way the rainbows looked over Potato Canyon," Karen added.

Karen and her husband Dan lived in New Mexico for thirty-three years and built a homestead between Pie Town and Datil along Highway 60. They eventually bought land and built a self-sufficient lifestyle. "I saw more people at the fire lookout than where we lived. We did it all, built roads, water and power systems, fences, gardens, and it was a good life," replied Karen about her homestead in New Mexico.

"Apply, volunteer if necessary but spend at least one summer working as a fire lookout if you enjoy the outdoors," suggested Karen about the fire lookout experience, "For those who land a first time lookout job, be sure and study your maps, learn your country, always be professional on the radio and laugh later be serious now," advised Karen.

Cindy loved her lookout perch in the Sandia Mountains on the edge of Albuquerque. "In 1992 Cedro Lookout became available, and I decided to apply for the position. The next thing I knew I was fourteen miles from home overlooking the East Mountain area. Seventeen years later, I'm still watching, tracking and communicating for this area I call home and what an incredible experience it has been," she stated.

"Not only do I have an awesome view everyday when I come to work, but I have the other lookouts as co-workers. Between all of us we can see the state from the Lincoln NF to the west and the Arizona border and from the Santa NF to the White Sands," she pointed out.

Cindy felt working as a lookout was a lot more than just having a good view and hanging out with nature. Cedro being a working lookout was responsible for an area consisting mainly of the urban interface where homes were at risk.

She explained, "The Sandia Mountains are made up of homes belonging to family, friends, colleagues and tax payers who pay my wage. The job consists of tracking everything that goes on in the East Mountain area, and understanding the language of two different agencies. I monitor both Forest Service and Bernalillo County radios."

Cindy too retired her post but has good memories of her years as a fire lookout.

Original Withington Fire Lookout
U.S. Forest Service Photo

Anne Ravenstone & Mary Schultz
Photo--Author's Collection

The town of Mountainair, located along the foothills of the Manzano Mountains in central New Mexico, has become a popular location for artists and writers. For decades, many seeking an alternative path and lifestyle have relocated to the small town that began its history as a railroad stop along the Atchison, Topeka & Santa Fe railroad line.

This group of innovative people has been good for the town, as they have restored several of the original buildings making up the community, as well as, provided lectures, art exhibits, musicals, pottery, mosaic classes and more. This free-thinking group has become an integral part of the community and gained the respect of locals for the ways in which they have managed to work with the town and keep it alive.

Many of the towns along Highway 60 started to decline in the 1940s and again in the 1960s when the Atchison, Topeka & Santa Fe Railroad decided to downsize and closed half of their railroad depots along the Belen Cutoff route. Mountainair survived when other towns along the route died, and those having an interest in the arts deserve much of the credit. This group invested their own money and time into making Mountainair a center for artists and those involved in literary pursuits.

Artists and those interested in the arts joined together not only to have a place to show and sell their art, but also to help beautify the town. A group of mosaic artists under the direction of Tomas Wolf created unique mosaics they placed on different buildings throughout the town. Others planted flowers and shrubs along Broadway Street during the summer months.

An art gallery in Mountainair had long been the dream of Mary Schultz. In the beginning she had thought of a store named "100% Mountainair" where arts and crafts of local people could be combined with the Chamber of Commerce giving out information about the area.

Finally, a group of twelve artists met together in 1995 and formed Cibola Arts. They agreed the art gallery should become involved in community outreach programs and public relations as well as provide a location for artists to display and sell their artwork. Over one hundred guests attended Cibola Arts Grand Opening.

The idea of an art council was initiated by a Moriarty artist named Kim Mason. She was interested in making art programs available to children during the summer months. She discovered that by forming an art council, the group might be able to obtain assistance from the NM Arts Commission. In 1994, Mason created the Torrance County Arts Council.

By the summer of 1995, Mason was looking for someone to take over the council and wondered if Cibola Arts might be interested. The Cibola Arts group was not sure they could take on anything new since they had only been in existence for four months. But, Mary set up a meeting at the Humming Bird Café in Mountainair and found there was an interest in having an art council also. The group accepted the responsibility of the Torrance County Art Council and named Mary its president. As the years passed, the art council became more of a Mountainair based organization and decided to change its name to the Manzano Mountain Art Council.

***

There are many people who have worked to make the Manzano Mountain Art Council a success during its fourteen year history. Dale Harris and David Poole have also been members since the early years of the organization. Other than Mary, those who have served as president are: Wray Simmons, Roy Kirby, Shirley Simmons, Bert Hermann, Wieland Elstner and Gayle Van Horn.

Yet, there are two women who have been more than instrumental in making the Manzano Mountain Art Council a success: Mary Schultz and Anne Ravenstone. The two met when Anne moved to the area from Minnesota and was working as a waitress at the Shaffer Hotel & Restaurant and living in Mountainair. They soon became friends and neighbors and over the years they have worked on countless art shows and projects together.

Mary was born in Quincy, Illinois and spent her childhood in Champaign-Urbana, Chicago and Tallahassee, Florida. When she moved with her mother to Florida it was the first time she had encountered segregation and it was hard for her to accept the practice even as a child. She asked her mother why African-Americans were treated so differently in Florida. Her mother told her, "That is just the way it is here."

Mary and her mother would move to Cincinnati, Ohio in 1952 and Mary explains about this time in her life, "Cincinnati was a relief in many ways. I was coming to the end of sixth grade and arrived at an old school with a few wonderful teachers," she stated. "I fit right in and made friends and thrived on the life there. I went through high school and toward the end of high school discovered that I could go on to college and study Interior Design."

**Mary as a student at the University of Cincinnati in 1962
Mary Schultz Photo**

Mary attended the University of Cincinnati and it was everything she had hoped for in obtaining a first-class education and preparing for a career in design. "The work was hard, tedious and challenging. Also unique in its incorporation of work and study life, as we were full time employees in alternate periods of time," she explained. "I graduated from the University of Cincinnati with a degree in Interior Design in 1963 and went to work for an interior design firm."

Mary married Roger Schultz in 1964 who was a classmate at the university. They lived in Cincinnati until the summer of 1966 when they discovered the enchantment of Santa Fe and the Sangre de Cristo Mountains. They had enjoyed their life in Cincinnati but soon found Santa Fe was where they wanted to live. They restored two places and built a house on a mountain. Mary would start doing design work again in 1975.

Mary's son Eric was born in Santa Fe in 1968. Mary tells a little about the experience, "Eric was born at the Catholic Maternity Institute which was a marvelous place. It was run by the medical mission sisters who were mid-wives and had a mid-wife training center there." Mary and Roger would divorce while they were living in Santa Fe.

Mary had her own interior design business in Santa Fe from 1978-2000. She was also involved with the Santa Fe Chamber of Commerce and was on the board of the Community Foundation. "It was a full, active and very rewarding time for me," Mary pointed out about her years in Santa Fe. "I also started a tutoring program in the local school system that evolved into the Partners in Education Program of the Community Foundation."

Mary met Lee Elder in 1980 and they have lived together ever since. Although satisfied with their lives in Santa Fe, they had a friend who owned land near Mountainair and he described its landscape so often that they decided to take a drive to Mountainair and check out the land. They bought land in what is now referred to as Loma Parda west of Mountainair where they hoped to build a weekend getaway.

They spent the summer of 1989 on the land in a small trailer with few conveniences. Mary described the experience, "We bought 80 acres and decided to spend the summer out there. We rented our house to the Santa Fe Opera and had about ten weeks to look forward to spending on the land," she stated. "It was a magical, mystical summer living in a small trailer watching the sun, moon, stars, ravens, swallows and jays. I kept up my design work in Santa Fe and we had every intention of returning at the end of the summer."

But, another piece of land became available that the couple liked even better and they would purchase the King place by the end of the summer. "Just arriving at the King place brought us into an area we had not seen all summer and in fact had no idea existed. Trees! Tall trees, beautiful trees and a house that was so intriguing."

The couple did not intend to permanently move to Mountainair yet, as they were still very involved with activities in Santa Fe. But, the peacefulness of the land would change their minds. "Even as we prepared to sell our house and as I relocated all my resource materials to the location, I really did not think I was leaving my life and work in Santa Fe," she stated.

But, they would leave Santa Fe in 1990, when they moved to their land among the ponderosa pine trees, and they have never left. Mary continued to work another five years on design work in Santa Fe before devoting her time to the Cibola Arts Gallery and Manzano Art Council.

In later years, Mary has branched out and collected unique beads from around the world and strung into wonderful creations she sells at Cibola Arts.

***

Anne Ravenstone has spent the majority of her life working as an artist in one art form or another. She explained how dance became her first love, "I was always an artist to some degree. I sang and played the piano all through high school and then found my real passion in college when I majored in Modern Dance," Anne explained.

Her family moved around during her childhood and growing up years, "I was a Texan until I was eight, then a Coloradoan until I was twenty-one, then a Minnesotan until I was forty-six and have been a New Mexican ever since," Anne stated.

While living in Minnesota Anne became involved with the professional Nancy Hauser Dance Company and School in Minneapolis. Over the years, she became one of their primary teachers and would eventually join the dance company. She toured the Midwest with the company and even performed as far away as Japan and Taiwan. "After leaving the company, I received numerous grants to present my own dance works and eventually presented a full concert of my choreography. I was an artist-in-residence in many communities throughout the state," Anne pointed out.

**Anne performing for the Nancy Hauser Dance Company--
Anne Ravenstone Photo**

Although, Anne loved to dance, she realized she had to
think about opportunities for aging dancers as she became
older. She thought the Southwest would be a good area to
start over and see if her knowledge of dance and her skills
were needed. She moved to New Mexico in 1993 and
discovered Mountainair.

She explained how she was able to continue with her
dancing moves, "For the first eleven years I lived in
Mountainair I had a dance studio at the old elementary school
on Highway 55 which was then owned by artists," she
explained. "I taught a weekly class for "mature" folks and did
several performances at the schoolhouse."

It has always been a challenge to make a living in small
communities throughout New Mexico, especially as the town
was coming out of a recession when Anne first arrived in
town, "Early on I thought I would make hand-dipped candles.
I had a chance to take a tin class which I thought might lead to
making candle holders. What it led to was a whole new
direction of becoming a decorative tin artist."

Before long, Anne became a respected wood and tin artist. She explained, "I have always loved weathered wood so I soon was creating functional pieces that partnered the tin and wood, developing a distinct style for myself," she pointed out. She incorporates her knowledge of movement and space learned during her dance years in her current artwork. Her work has been shown and sold in Santa Fe, Socorro, Carrizozo, Belen, Tome, Albuquerque and of course at Cibola Arts in Mountainair.

Anne has also worked for many years as an educator with the Mountainair Public Schools in an after-school program. "For many years I administered a large after-school program that had both academic and art classes in the curriculum. The program has been cut to a small after-school art program in more recent years."

After her retirement from Mountainair Public Schools, Anne has become more involved in the Manzano Mountain Art Council and eventually was elected as its president. The number of artists and programs has significantly risen under Anne and Mary's leadership skills and become an important part of the community and its history.

Anne explained her reasons why she will always be involved in art in some manner. "The importance of a strong community is a focus for me at this point in my life. I mainly work at helping build that strong community through the arts as that is what I know best," she stated. "I believe the arts have much to offer the town in terms of economic benefit, beautification and feeding the souls of its residents."

***

Marilyn Conway with her camera at five years old
Marilyn Conway Photo

Another artist who has lived near Mountainair for almost three decades and spent a lifetime working as an artist and photographer, is Marilyn Conway. Marilyn's love for photography began when she received her first Brownie camera at the age of five years old. Marilyn's father was a commercial artist and it was natural for him to give his young daughter lessons on light, color and composition. Her dad had a home art studio and Marilyn said, "I used to drive my father crazy getting into his paints and brushes and often ruining an expensive brush. As I got older, my dad taught me to use his camera and took me to numerous museums and art galleries. He was constantly giving me art lessons, so I was primed to become an artist."

Marilyn was born in East Orange, New Jersey and moved to the suburbs of Woodbridge, NJ when she was ten years old. Her parents built a house on her grandparents' property. "My grandparents had chickens, ducks, lots of fruit trees, and huge vegetable gardens. My grandmother had a fabulous flower garden and sold bouquets of flowers to the neighbors for one dollar each. My grandmother always had me pick the bouquets."

Marilyn graduated from the prodigious Parson's School of Design in New York City. One of her professors at Parsons was offered a visiting partnership at the University of New Mexico art department for one year. He brought five of his students from Parsons, including Marilyn, with him to UNM. Marilyn graduated with a Bachelor of Fine Arts from UNM.

She fell in love with New Mexico and met her future husband, Terry Conway, while he was a graduate student at the art department at UNM. He would later teach at the University of South Carolina and the University of Wisconsin where Marilyn also took classes and had her first photography shows.

Marilyn and her husband would eventually divorce, and she would devote her time to her daughter Phoebe, working as a potter, working in her darkroom and running a Youth Program at Martineztown House of Neighborly Service in downtown Albuquerque. "Working in Martineztown in the 1970s and 80s was so much fun. We took the kids all over New Mexico—week long camping trips to Taos and the Sandia Mountains; we toured Carlsbad Caverns, Acoma, and the Salinas Missions; and went swimming at Blue Water and Manzano Lakes. I took lots of photographs of the kids on these trips with my old 2 ¼ Mamaya camera and am in the process of scanning all the negatives to put them in a self-published book."

In the early 1990s, Marilyn ran the recreation program at Carrie Tingley Children's Hospital in Albuquerque for five years and then in the mid-1990s decided to make her living entirely with her photography skills.

At one point, she decided to try and photograph every town in New Mexico. She had come through Mountainair many times to take photos of this area. She liked the community and the land west of town where she would eventually settle.

Her long time partner, Joe Minella, helped her build her house. The first year they poured cement, and the second year they framed the house. They would go on to build the house over a five year period, and then hire local builder Nick DiMeglio to finish the house.

Marilyn has won numerous awards and grants throughout her distinguished career as an artist. Among her awards was the Willard Van Dyke Memorial Grant awarded by the New Mexico Council on Photography in Santa Fe. Her photographs are in permanent collections of the Museum of Albuquerque, New Mexico Museum of Art in Santa Fe, UNM Hospital, Intel Corporation, NM Arts in Public places, the Billy Graham Museum plus many banks and corporations. She has had photo exhibitions in New Mexico, Arizona, Texas and California. She sells her stock photo images around the world online through Getty Images.

In a 1990s photo (pictured), Marilyn poses with one of her hand colored Route 66 Photographs on an Albuquerque Transit Bus

***

Much of the credit of attracting the first artists and writers to New Mexico goes to socialite Mabel Dodge Luhan who discovered Taos shortly after the turn of the twentieth century and never wanted to live anywhere else thereafter.

Luhan was the heiress to a wealthy Buffalo, New York banker and grew up among the socially elite. She attended a school for girls until she was sixteen then had another year of schooling in New York City before touring Europe in 1896. Next, she attended the infamous Chevy Chase finishing school in Washington, D.C. when she returned from her European tour.

She married in secret at the age of 21 because her father did not approve of her marrying Karl Evans, the son of a steamboat owner. The couple would have one son, before Karl was killed in a hunting accident two and a half years after their marriage. Her family decided to send her to Paris and later that year she married Edwin Dodge, a wealthy architect.

Mabel and Edwin lived in Florence from 1905 until 1912. She often entertained artists and writers in their home. The Dodge's moved to New York in 1912 and Mabel found an apartment in Greenwich Village. Before long she became known as a patron of the arts and held weekly salons in her apartment.

Next, she would marry Maurice Sterne. Sterne moved into a cottage behind the main house where Dodge lived. Upon her arrival, she developed a literary colony. D.H. Lawrence and his wife Frieda visited Mabel as well as other influential artists and poets.

Her marriage to Sterne started to unravel when they moved to Taos. Mabel was more interested in the traditions of the area and the people than Sterne. She also had met a Pueblo Indian from Taos named Tony Luhan and her life would never be the same. Luhan set up a tepee in front of the house where she was living and drummed until she came out to meet him.

Sterne threatened shooting Luhan, but Mabel sent him away and never lived with him again but continued to support him for four more years until divorcing him. Luhan would become the love of Mabel's life and she never needed another man after they were married. They would spend the remainder of their lives together in Taos. Mabel passed away at her home in Taos in 1962. The Mabel Dodge Luhan House is a National Landmark and an historic inn and conference center.

Mabel Dodge Luhan is credited with starting the art movement in New Mexico. Because of her Georgia O'Keeffe and others would visit her in her historic house in Taos and discover New Mexico. Many soon found their own house or piece of land and allowed the enchantment of New Mexico to influence their paintings and writings about the area. Mabel's hospitality was known throughout the area and she was instrumental in helping others to discover the beauty of Taos and New Mexico.

Epilogue

Since childhood I have been interested in the outlaw history of the American West. While taking New Mexico History back in the seventh grade, our class visited the site of the Lincoln County Wars where Billy the Kid made a name for himself. This would start my interest in the history of the American Frontier and the independent characters making up its history. I often retuned to Lincoln after that first visit and even lived there for a year while teaching history at Hondo High School. I always loved the atmosphere of the town and the frontier spirit found there.

But, more than the outlaw history making up the history of the frontier, I found myself wanting to know more about their wives, girlfriends and mothers. How did this affect their lives? How did they really feel knowing the man in their life was an outlaw and might be apprehended or killed any day? Why did these women fall in love with outlaws in the first place? Why were they so different from other women of their era?

While working as the Curator of the Crook County Museum in Sundance, Wyoming in the 1990s, I often explained the history of Larry Longabaugh alias the Sundance Kid. The first time he was incarcerated was in the Crook County Jail in 1883 and since that time the town has used his name as a calling card to lure tourists to the picturesque community at the base of Sundance Mountain in northeast Wyoming?

Several members of the Hole-in-the-Wall Gang had lasting relationships with women. When I discovered the Sundance Kid married a woman who went by the alias of Etta Place, I wanted to know more about her life and relationship with the man who would become an infamous outlaw. But, so far no historian or researcher has discovered the true identity of Etta Place or found any information on her past and eventual demise.

The first the American public knew of Etta Place was from the files of the Pinkerton Detective Agency hoping to apprehend the outlaw gang. She was most often referred to as Mrs. Place or Mrs. Longabaugh and went by a variety of names: Rita, Ethel and Eva were three but she most often was called Etta.

In 1902, Etta went to a New York City hospital and the Pinkerton Agency was able to get one of the first descriptions of the woman who was often seen at Sundance's side. She was described as being either 23 or 24 years old and had a medium complexion and dark hair. She had either blue or gray eyes and possessed no distinguishing marks or blemishes. The Pinkerton Detectives named her Ethel Place.

Etta Place had been in Sundance's life for a decade before the Pinkerton's knew of her existence. They were surprised to discover a woman had accompanied the Sundance Kid to Argentina. Around the same time, they discovered the famous photograph of the Sundance Kid and Etta Place taken in a New York City studio. Many historians suspect this was their wedding photo but no one has proven it yet.

There are several theories as to Etta's identity. She may have been a rancher's daughter from either Denver or Texas, as she knew how to shoot and load a gun and was an accomplished horse-back rider. But, the Pinkerton Detectives most often associated her past with the state of Texas.

Etta may have been a high-classed prostitute and worked in parlor houses in San Antonio, Texas, one of which was Fanny Porter's Hell's Half Acre. The Sundance Kid and his outlaw friends often stopped at the parlor house. Women who worked in these houses guarded their identities and always went by a nickname. She may have gone by the name of Ethel Bishop while working in the profession.

Etta Place and the Sundance Kid left the United States and headed for Buenos Aires, Argentina in the spring of 1901. Butch Cassidy would meet them there later, and they would establish a successful ranch and attempt going straight. But, the Pinkerton Detectives did not give up easily and distributed wanted posters throughout Argentina and South America.

Sundance Kid & Etta Place
Photo--Author's Collection

The Pinkerton's discovered the trail of Sundance and Etta once again in New York City in April of 1902. The couple stayed at a rooming house while they vacationed and saw relatives. They even visited Cooney Island and hung out on the beach like typical tourists. Sundance introduced Etta to his relatives as his wife.

Some writers think Sundance and Etta came back to the United States so he could see a medical doctor. But, Etta had medical problems too, and maybe she was the one who needed to see a doctor. According to the Pinkerton records, the couple visited back and forth between the United States and South America quite often. They visited the St. Louis World Fair in 1904.

By 1905, Butch and Sundance had returned to a life of crime when men fitting their descriptions robbed a bank in Rio Gallegos, Argentina. Soon, news articles were flying between the United States and Argentina pointing out the exploits of the two outlaws.

Once again, Etta's existence shadows their activities. We know Etta was still living in South America in 1907, but her whereabouts becomes obscured in the years thereafter. She may have returned to the United States either to have an appendectomy or to give birth to a child, but neither theory has been proven.

It seems Etta was having some type of medical issue, as she and Sundance returned to the United States and consulted a medical doctor once again in 1907. She may have died in childbirth in a Denver hospital, as Sundance returned to South America after shooting up his room and drinking heavily the night before. This was the only time he sailed without her.

Etta may have become discontented and decided to remain in the United States. But, Sundance can be credited with protecting her identity until the end. Butch Cassidy and the Sundance Kid died in a shoot-out with the Bolivian army after robbing a mine payroll shipment in 1908. If Etta Place was still alive, she must have mourned when she heard the news.

Way too often in the research I have conducted on women's history, I have found wonderful photographs of women with no identification or even a hint to the woman's past. Etta Place may have not wanted her identity discovered, while the identities of other women were lost due to negligence.

It is often impossible to discover a person's identity without a name or date. It is important to label family photographs so the history will not be forgotten. We have already lost way too many stories about the first women pioneers; as well as, women currently making history.

***

As in the case of Etta Place, the identities of many women who lived and prospered in frontier communities will never be discovered or remembered, as would the facts making up my Grandma Agnes' life if I had not searched for information and requested old photographs from my relatives' photo collections.

She was only ten years old in this photograph and still had her whole life ahead of her, but a little over twenty-five years later she would pass away leaving her children orphaned at the end of the Great Depression. This happened often during the early years of frontier settlement when children were left when their parents died of an illness, were killed by Native Americans or outlaws or had a tragic accident.

Agnes Jones in 1915—Photo--Author's Collection

Grandma Agnes lived with her father when her parents divorced. Her father would remarry and they would move to Los Angeles. Agnes grew up as a city girl and attended San Pedro High School. She would become accustomed to the ocean breezes and city lights. Yet, she would fall in love with a man more than ten years her senior who wanted to be a cowboy and have his own cattle ranch in New Mexico.

Grandma Agnes passed away before I was born. Yet, I have often thought about her and wondered how she felt about living in the deserts of New Mexico after growing up near the Pacific Ocean. In all the photos I have seen of her she appears happy, except for one of her sitting on the porch of the ranch house near Cuervo with her children shortly after her husband's death. She had a look of sadness and despair in her eyes as she gazes into the camera that long ago day.

When Charles, Agnes' husband and my grandfather passed away in 1939, it would throw the family into chaos. Agnes was unable to hold onto the ranch, and she made a desperate decision to trade it for a gas station in Cuervo. She was hoping she and the kids could run the station and somehow manage to support themselves in the process. They found refuge in the old schoolhouse in town and tried to put their lives back together after the death of Charles.

But, Agnes would have medical problems a few years later and pass away one rainy morning when she was only thirty-six years old leaving four small children with no one to care for them. Neighbors and friends took in the children, arranged Agnes' funeral and contacted relatives in Kansas to see if anyone could give the children a home. The day of Agnes' funeral was sad for everyone. The rains were continuous the week before she was laid to rest in the Cuervo Cemetery. Her coffin was loaded into the back of a wagon and pulled by horses to the cemetery while family and friends walked behind.

My father saved a small Bible once belonging to Grandma Agnes and a piece of her wedding dress he kept tucked inside the Bible. He also had their wedding photo that we often took out and passed around while discussing their lives. They seemed happy as they stood next to one another in her father's backyard in California. Agnes was only sixteen and Charles twenty-nine when they married. They would have six children, two girls and four boys.

They would eventually settle on land south of Cuervo on New Mexico's east side. Agnes spent weeks alone with the children on their isolated ranch while Charles worked away from home. He built dirt tanks for ranchers in the area who wanted to capture the flow from the summer monsoon season and had a small, cattle and horse herd. She had chickens that she took care of and a garden to supplement their food supply.

I wish I had known Grandma Agnes. I am sure she would have been a wonderful grandmother. I will never know her in the way I knew my grandmother on my mother's side of the family. I have no idea what type of music she liked, if she read books or what were her interests and hobbies.

The cap-rock making up much of New Mexico's eastern plains where Agnes and Charles settled is still big, isolated ranch country. I doubt the land has changed much since Agnes arrived in New Mexico as a young bride with her aspirations of being a rancher's wife close to a century ago. Grandma Agnes never made the pages of history books, but she will always remain in the hearts of her family and descendants.

Yet, Grandma Agnes was the typical woman who lived on the American Frontier. She took care of her family and made her mark on the community where she lived; and she died young as was the case of a large percentage of women on the frontier. The American West was often a hard place for women, but many of their stories have survived in diaries, letters and family histories giving us a hint of their pasts.

***

I want to include one final story about an exceptional young woman who would have made history if she had been given the chance. In the mid-1980s, I taught history and coached volleyball at Hondo High School. Hondo is a small village between Ruidoso and Roswell in the foothills of the Sacramento Mountains. One weekend in February of 1988, a member of my volleyball team was murdered. Even though almost three decades have passed since her death, her murder continues to remain an unsolved mystery.

Her name was Katrina Chavez, and when she died she was sixteen years old and a sophomore at Hondo High School. She was an intelligent and motivated young woman who had her entire life ahead of her until someone took it all away. She was buried in her basketball uniform in the Hondo Cemetery across the street from the school, while her friends, teachers and family gave her an emotional farewell.

On the day she died, her basketball coach was to stop by and pick her up and they were going to Cloudcroft where Katrina had won an important basketball award. When her coach arrived at her house, the front door was open and one of her basketball shoes was on the front porch. It appeared there had been a scuffle. He looked and looked for her and called her name for over an hour, but she failed to show or answer. Everyone knew this was not like Katrina, something had happened or she would have been waiting there for the coach as she said she would do, as she had always been reliable and dependable.

The police were notified and search crews organized. The following day, Katrina's body was found along the banks of the Rio Hondo River. She had been strangled and drowned. In the investigation, it was determined that she probably knew her attacker. He or she had chased her up and down the river bank. There were several places where signs of a fight had occurred. She had fought back, and even gotten away a couple times, but her attackers were eventually able to overcome her.

The second week of the investigation, a fellow student was arrested for the murder and taken into custody. He had been seen at the time of Katrina's death walking up from the river. His pants were soaked and he was distracted and crying. When he was interviewed about the incident he swore over and over he had not been involved, but he appeared to know more than he was telling. He and Katrina had known one another all their lives and had played together as children.

A teacher at the school was also questioned. He was teaching a self-defense course after school where his students learned how to do strangle holds similar to the one that helped to kill Katrina. The student taken into custody was taking this class. The teacher was not rehired at the school and quit before the school year was over. He was questioned extensively by the police but no arrests were made and he soon moved to another state.

In the months following Katrina's death, the student taken into custody was released for lack of evidence. There were no other suspects, and soon the years went by and nothing more was heard about finding the person who murdered Katrina. Someone knows what happened that tragic day, but so far they are not talking.

I will never forget the happy, volleyball player who had such a positive outlook on life. She refused to give up and inspired the other team members to feel the same. She had a "funny" personality and kept the team laughing. She was mischievous and liked to play practical jokes. The situation is so unfair, but there are thousands of people in New Mexico who have lost loved ones in this manner and after fifty years are still waiting for answers.

She would be in her mid-forties now if she had been allowed to live. I am sure she would have a family and children and maybe even be teaching, coaching and inspiring her own team. But, Katrina resides in a grave across the street from Hondo High School. When I pass through Hondo, I always stop and clean the weeds off Katrina's grave and put a few flowers on her tombstone. It seems not many people stop by anymore and it makes me sad. I can still conjure an image of her when we won our first volleyball game and she spun me around the gymnasium in her excitement.

Throughout my twenty year career as a high school teacher, I had students die in car accidents but Katrina was the only one murdered. Her murder has haunted me all these years. Her final hours were terrifying, and I am sure she was more frightened than she had ever been in her life, as I know I would have been. She tried to get away. She was strong and could outrun most of the boys in her class. I still wonder why Katrina or "Kat-Brat" as we often called her was the one targeted that day. Hopefully someday someone will come forth with new information on the case, as I would hate to see her short life be totally forgotten.

Katrina Chavez — No. 6-- Standing next to the Author in 1987--Photo--Author's Collection

***

Women's history helped to shape the settlement of the American West where the rules of the Victorian era did not always apply. Wyoming was the first state to give women the right to vote and women growing up on the frontier were considered more unconventional than in the more settled areas of the country. Women were often praised for their independent spirits and business sense.

Without the women the frontier would have continued in its wicked ways and violent interactions. There would have been few churches and schools, courthouses and other signs of civilization. Men may have outnumbered the women, but the women were the backbone of the communities where they lived. Most of the stories about adventuresome women need to be told, because as each generation passes more and more of their stories are being lost.

Book Cover
Unidentifed women hikers in the 1920s
Photo-Author's Collection

References

Adair, Cornelia. *My Diary*. Austin, Texas: University of Texas Press, 1965.

Butler, Anne M. *Daughters of Joy, Sisters of Misery Prostitutes in the American West 1865-90*. Urbana and Chicago: University of Illinois Press, 1987.

Flood, Renee Sansom. *Lost Bird of Wounded Knee: Spirit of the Lakota*. New York: Scribner Press, 1995.

Boone, Seaman, Frances. *Nehasane Fire Observer: An Adirondack Woman's Summer of '42*. Utica, New York: Nicholas K. Burns Publishing.

Chamberlain, Kathleen P. *In the Shadow of Billy the Kid: Susan McSween and the Lincoln County War*. Albuquerque: University of New Mexico Press, 2013.

Chindahl, George Leonard. *History of the Circus in America*. Published in 1952.

Frost, Gordon H. *The Gentlemen's Club the Story of Prostitution in El Paso*. El Paso, Texas: Mangan Books, 1983.

Geist, Valerius. *Buffalo National History and Legend of North American Bison*. Stillwater, Minnesota: Voyageur Press, 1996.

Gipson, Fred. *The Cow Killers with the Afosa Commission in Mexico*. Austin, Texas: University of Texas Press, 1956.

Jordan, Teresa. *Cowgirls: Women of the American West an Oral History.* New York: Anchor Books, 1984.

Katz, William Loren. *Black Women of the Old West.* New York: Ethrac Publications, Inc., 1995.

Lecompte, Mary Lou. *Cowgirls of the Rodeo – Pioneer Professional Athletes.* Urbana & Chicago: University of Illinois Press, 1993.

Lenski, Lois. *Indian Captive the story of Mary Jamison.* New York: Harper-Collins Children's Books, 1969.

Luhan, Mabel Dodge. *Edge of the Taos Desert an Escape to Reality.* Albuquerque: University of New Mexico Press, Fourth Printing 1993.

MacKell, Jan. *Red Light Women of the Rocky Mountains.* Albuquerque: University of New Mexico Press, 2009.

Massey, Sara R. *Texas Women on the Cattle Trails.* College Station, Texas: Texas A & M University, 2006.

Mifflin, Margot. *The Blue Tattoo the Life of Olive Oatman.* Lincoln: University of Nebraska Press, 2009.

Moore, Jo. *Article on the history of El Bosque.*

Seagraves, Anne. *Soiled Doves Prostitution in the Early West.* Hayden, Idaho: Wesanne Publications, 1994.

Stratton, R.B. *Captivity of the Oatman Girls.* Lincoln, Nebraska: University of Nebraska, Press, 1983.

Torrance County History Book.

West, Beverly. *More than Petticoats Remarkable New Mexico Women.* Guilford, Connecticut: The Globe Pequot Press, 2001.

Newspaper Article. *My Mother, Maud Medders* by John E. Wright. *Torrance County Citizen,* October 1981.

Article: *A Novel Experiment: Hallie Comes to Eddy's Gulch. Women in Forestry Magazine,* 1983.

Campaign in Mexico against Food-and-Mouth Disease, 1947-52. United States Department of Agriculture Agricultural Research Service, Washington, D.C. 1954.

Personal Interview with Lucille Mathews Boyle Reynolds in April of 2016.

Personal Interview with Barbara Mathews in April of 2016.

Personal Interview with Anne Ravenstone in May of 2016.

Personal Interview with Mary Schultz in May of 2016.

Personal Interview with Marilyn Conway in August of 2016.

Unidentified Woman and Dog Friend

Made in the USA
Columbia, SC
31 March 2018